Writing Better

A Simple Rhetorical Guide to Process, Structure, & Coherence

David L. Rogers

Writing Better Essays

A Simple Rhetorical Guide
to Process, Structure,
& Coherence

David L. Rogers

Kingston University Press

Kingston University Press
Kingston University
Penrhyn Road
Kingston upon Thames
Surrey, KT1 2EE

British Library Cataloguing in Publication Data available.
ISBN: 978-1-899999-61-3
Typeset by PK Editorial (www.pkeditorial.co.uk)

Printed in the UK by Lightning Source
Cover design: Nastasiya Alyakisheva
(nastasiya.alyakisheva@gmail.com)
Internal illustration of mind maps and diagrams by Pin-Ju Chen
(www.pinjuchen.com, email: jujuchen01@hotmail.com)

Dedicated to Lindsay, Lily, and Joe

With thanks to students of Kingston University, London

Contents

INTRODUCTION

Our Process: A Mastermind Approach

"Think of writing as a process on its way to a
product."
> (Richard Marius, *A Writer's Companion*, 3rd ed.)[1]

"Writers have to view their ideas objectively so they can
experience their writing as a reader would. Being
objective in this way requires some role playing, like that
in conversation."
> (Collete Dalute, "Do Writers Talk to Themselves?,"
> in Sarah Warshauer Freedman, ed., *The Acquisition
> of Written Language: Response and Revision*)[2]

This is a book about essay writing. Its easy-to-follow stages and
simple rhetorical principles will help you develop a reliable
process for structuring your argumentative essays coherently
and persuasively. All writers need a reliable process if they hope
to write successful essays, whatever the type and whatever their
discipline. Generally speaking, however, inexperienced writers,
including students when they arrive at university, have not
developed any process at all, much less one that they can trust
repeatedly. For that reason, they typically sit down at their
computer, sometimes with a plan, but often without one, and
they start to write. Having begun, they continue until they reach
their word limit or express a conclusion, whichever comes first.
They then submit their essay – and suffer the consequences.

But no one consistently writes good, persuasive essays in
one sitting, however much or little planning she may have done.
Good writing always requires active thinking, considered
revision, and, sometimes, a rearrangement of parts. Ultimately,
all good writing is synonymous with rewriting, with a process of
drafting, which this book will provide for you. You may want to
adapt this process once you get the hang of it. Indeed, I will
encourage you to do just that so that your final process suits

9

your style, temperament, and situation. Or you may eventually choose to abandon it altogether for a different type of process all of your own. Yet you will always need a process, and the one that I will explain in this book works. I guarantee it.

We might refer to this process as a mastermind approach. *Mastermind* is a long-running English game show on which contestants are asked to answer a series of questions about a range of topics. Each has two minutes to answer his set of questions. The first Master of Ceremonies Magnus Magnusson coined a trademark comment that he repeated whenever a bell signaled the end of each contestant's time while he was in the middle of asking a question. "I've started, so I'll finish," he would say, and the approach that many novice essayists use displays a similar determination. Once they have begun to write or type their essays, with or without any initial planning, once they have "started," they continue to write or type until they have "finished."

As we will see, the advantage to students who take such a determined approach is that they often instinctively write themselves to a conclusion. They often express this conclusion in a sentence or two at the end of the essay, sometimes even announcing it with the phrase "In conclusion." The disadvantage, however, is that run-of-the-mill mastermind conclusions are notoriously hard to understand in the context of the ideas that precede them. More often than not, they read more like a final assertion or a surprise ending for a short story than a well-supported contention. As a consequence, they are seldom as convincing as they should be. They may be engaging. They may be intelligent and valid. They may even connect implicitly to what has been a somewhat coherent argument. But the way in which they appear obscures this fact and undermines their effectiveness.

The reason for this ineffectiveness is reasonably simple. Mastermind essays are essentially linear in structure. Readers can, therefore, really make sense of their conclusions only by returning to the start of the essays and reading them again. With these second readings, they know the conclusions of the arguments from the beginning. But we cannot expect our readers to take such time with our essays. So we must heed the advice of Dalute above and assume the role of the reader for ourselves, reading our mastermind essays impartially as part of our process. When we do, we will experience for ourselves how the act of re-reading our essays serves to re-structure them. The analyses and arguments that had previously preceded our conclusions will now support and explain explicit statements of them.

I will, however, ask you to add a second step to the role-playing that Dalute recommends. After reading our mastermind essays, we will physically copy and paste explicit expressions of our conclusions at the top. By 'sandwiching' the principal content of our drafts – the body of our essays – between two articulations of our conclusions, one at the beginning and the other at the end, we will establish for ourselves the characteristic structure for strong argumentative essays and draft its crucial element: an explicit *thesis*. We will also transform the role of our mastermind essays. No longer will they remain the final product of our writing, the essays that we submit. Instead they will become a means to our end, a key stage in our new drafting process, but only a stage.

Don't worry right now if this simple relocation of your conclusion-as-thesis initially seems a slightly odd step to take. I will explain and exemplify it and all of the stages in our process in the chapters that follow. Don't be concerned about how your readers may respond to reading a version of your mastermind conclusion at the start of your final essay. You may have been warned that repeating yourself in essays implies a lack of respect towards your readers or, worse, potentially casts you as a simpleton. However, successful writing negates that warning. So too does the experience of anyone who reads a lot of student essays. The best practice of experienced writers (professional and advanced students alike) shows that, paradoxically, the most persuasive place to state your conclusions is not at the end of your essays (that is, not *only* at the end), but near the beginning. The structure of the best argumentative essays, it turns out, is *circular* and *reiterative*.

There is something reassuring about such a structure. As with written essays, the fundamental structure for persuasive conversation is also very often circular and reiterative. Most people, it seems, intuitively begin their verbal responses by stating the crux of their belief, the thesis they hold about the topic in question. They then explain the reasons why they believe what they want to persuade their listeners to accept. Once they have, they almost inevitably, and perhaps unconsciously, repeat an approximation of their thesis just before they stop talking. It is as if we all know that it's wise to remind our listeners of our thesis one last time before we finish, and so we restate it before we conclude. And, since you probably duplicate this structure when you respond orally to questions, it ought to be second nature for you to create the same one for your argumentative essays.

To help you, I have set out the defining structure of a strong argumentative essay below.

Formal Introductory Paragraph:

Leading to and including

Mastermind Conclusion Refined as Thesis

Body of Essay:

Argument:

Analysis & Supporting Evidence

(Two Effective Organizational Structures: General to Specific or Specific to General, Least Important to Most Important)

Final Paragraph:

Including

Revised Version of Mastermind Conclusion

Our Methods: Rhetoric and Imitation

"Rhetoric is the art or discipline that deals with the use of discourse, spoken or written, to inform or persuade or move an audience..."

(Edward P. J. Corbett, *Classical Rhetoric for the Modern Student*)[3]

"Whenever I read a book or a passage that particularly pleased me, in which a thing was said or an effect rendered with propriety, in which there was either some conspicuous force or some happy distinction in the style, I must sit down at once and set myself to ape that quality. I was unsuccessful, and I knew it; and tried again, and was again unsuccessful and always unsuccessful; but at least in these vain bouts, I got some practice in rhythm, in harmony, in construction and the co-ordination of parts... That, like it or not, is the way to learn to write; whether I have profited or not, that is the way."

(Robert Louis Stevenson, "A College Magazine," *Memories and Portraits*, cited in David Daiches, *Robert Louis Stevenson and his World*)[4]

The methods that inform our mastermind process for writing better argumentative essays rest on simple applications of classic rhetorical practice. As Corbett says, rhetoric engages us in either an "art" or "discipline" of persuasion, and the primary aim of all argumentative essayists is to persuade their readers. So any attempt to help you improve your powers of persuasion should, by definition, involve some understanding of rhetorical principles, which for us will include more "discipline" than "art." The techniques and devices I will stress won't be overly formal. Nor, as we have seen, will they require you to replace what comes naturally to you with any radically new approaches to your writing. For trying to persuade others comes to us almost as naturally as breathing. We encounter – and enact – rhetorical strategies of persuasion every day of our lives, both in conversation and in writing. Debates with our friends about music, films, sporting teams, and fashion are rhetorical. Newspaper editorials are rhetorical. So too are advertisements or book reviews, political debates or election slogans, and campaigns, as is someone writing argumentative essays or trying to convince her parents to buy her a car for graduation or give her some extra spending money for spring break.

In spite of the naturally pervasive nature of rhetoric in our lives, however, we can all improve our skills of essay writing, and one of our key aids for improvement will involve exercises of imitation. Throughout the book, I will identify good practice and ask you to copy it. As Stevenson, the Victorian who wrote the novel *Treasure Island* among other books, suggests in his personal confession about "apeing," the rationale behind such a strategy is straightforward and commonsensical. By actively imitating experienced writers, at first literally but then more freely and inventively, we don't just learn to distinguish how good writing works. We also experience its qualities as we type or write our imitations on the page. And, as we do, we gain an insight into our own style and habits (good and bad) and how to improve them. Most importantly, what we learn is more likely to stick.

Like rhetoric in general, our practice of imitation concentrates on what we should *do* rather than what we should *avoid* doing. It thus engages us in what is known as a positive discipline. This discipline began in Greece in the fifth century BC with a group of philosophers, including Aristotle, known as the Sophists. In those days, rhetorical training applied principally to public speaking (and was always restricted to boys), and Plato, one of the greatest Greek philosophers, had grave reservations about the practice of writing. The original speaker-turned-writer, Plato pointed out, could not always be present to explain and defend his meaning. As a consequence, writing was more open to misinterpretation, subject to distortion by any sceptical or inquisitive reader. Less reliable and so less truthful than speech, writing could not be trusted.

When we argue a thesis as a writer, in other words, we do not enjoy a second chance. To counter this disadvantage, we must be certain not only to structure our written arguments appropriately, but also to articulate them even more precisely and coherently than when we attempt to persuade someone orally. Otherwise, we can't expect to sway our readers. Contemporary readers, including university lecturers, lead very busy lives. They almost certainly won't take time to re-read what they do not easily understand or when they lose your point. They won't come to your aid as they read, no matter how much they may want you to succeed.

For this reason, you must take your writing seriously. Learning to write better, more persuasive essays requires concerted effort. Some people undoubtedly have an aptitude for writing. Writing comes more easily and naturally to some than it does to others. But writing an effective argumentative essay is a learned skill, a craft, and, like playing a musical instrument or mastering a sport such as tennis or diving, it entails a range of techniques. Yet anyone can learn to apply our techniques – if, that is, she is willing to work at them, to practice. So you will have to commit yourself to our idea of practice if you want to make the most of this book. With this commitment, you will not only learn the concepts behind these techniques, but you will also develop the ability to apply those techniques on the page – and in your speech. You will then derive more satisfaction from your writing and, if you are a student, earn better grades. You will have become a rhetorician of the right sort.

CHAPTER 1

Essay Writing as Process: A Few Simple Steps

> "[G]ood writers do not create wonderful texts in one smooth step. Rather, writers plan, compose, revise, throw drafts away, rewrite, and sometimes seem to do nothing at all. These processes do not simply involve expression. People express ideas in writing, but they also react to their texts. Writers read and critique their texts. They talk to themselves about ways to improve their writing."
>
> (Colette Dalute, "Do Writers Talk to Themselves?," in Sarah Warshauer Freedman, ed., *The Acquisition of Written Language: Response and Revision*)[5]

First Stages: Preparation as Part of Your Writing Process

Now that we have established the obligation to draft our essays, we can look at the complementary steps in our process that precede the actual writing of your mastermind drafts. Perhaps the biggest hurdle for writing good essays is time or, more accurately, the *lack* of it, and this problem is perhaps particularly acute for students. It's for this reason that, understandably, inexperienced essayists sometimes write their essays the night or even the morning before they are due. Occasionally, they may even get away with this strategy. But remember: consistently writing successful essays demands a series of stages of writing and revising. Good writing of any sort is always as much an exercise in re-writing, drafting, and re-drafting, as it is an inspirational taking-off.

STAGE 1

Procrastination
(*Not Always as Bad as You Might Think*)

For many good writers a reliable process of writing includes some form of procrastination. All of us, I'm sure, have found ourselves making an extra cup of something before sitting down to write our essays or washing dishes left over for days before we can settle at our computers or writing desks. Some famous writers have even invented eccentric routines for procrastinating as part of their process. The American novelist Ernest Hemingway, for example, reputedly had to sharpen all of the pencils that he thought he might use during the day before he could write his first words. Yet the important thing for Hemingway was that he procrastinated with a purpose, and for a purpose, which was to put himself in the right frame of mind to write. Procrastination was not, for Hemingway, a way to avoid writing. It served as the first stage in his overall process for thinking and writing, and, given how much Hemingway published and how long people have continued to read what he wrote, his purposeful procrastination evidently worked for him. He therefore teaches us that whether we procrastinate, or how we procrastinate, as part of our writing process matters less than whether we have any process at all. So don't think that you have to start writing your first drafts straight away. If you need first to put yourself in the right frame of mind, then find a way of procrastinating that feels natural. Then incorporate it into your process, as long, that is, as it does not serve as an excuse to avoid starting at all.

STAGE 2

Freewriting
(*An Early Generating Stage*)

The second stage in our process is equally as individual but even more liberating, and it should play an integral part of any writing process that you eventually deploy. We'll use the term *freewriting*, for it represents a stage in our process in which we can and should write with absolute freedom, with complete abandon, without caring about how good our writing is or how good our ideas are or whether we are convincing or correct. Freewriting doesn't tie us down to any established act, any format, any structure, or any style, and the practical values of freewriting are manifold. Essentially this stage gives you the green light to initiate your writing process without knowing for sure what you think about your topic or, perhaps, even what your topic is. (In fact it encourages you to start writing before you are certain what you think or how you want to express yourself.)

Freewriting, that is, doesn't demand any definite conclusion or formal result, just a 'letting go' during which the ideas you have (or, in many cases, those that you weren't aware that you had) can emerge. You can later manipulate them, re-structure them, mold them, much as a potter might work with clay or a painter with paint, rubbing out when necessary, painting over areas when she wants, or tearing the whole thing up and starting over when she desires. In this way, it gives you the chance to experience what we might call the 'genius' of writing, the unique ability of the act of writing to generate those specific ideas without which we would not hold those general assumptions that usually inform our freewriting in the first place, but which, were we to rely solely on trying to conjure them up in the abstract, in our heads, so to speak, would elude us, remain forever out of reach.

Although freewriting may not require us to have any defined aim in mind for our argumentative essays, you will, nevertheless, want to ensure that you have enough to say about your topic before you start, preferably by having done all of your assigned reading and some research, either online or in the library. That way, there will be fewer reasons for you to ponder as you write. Pondering is an unproductive method of procrastination whereas purposeful methods of procrastination, such as washing those dishes or sharpening those pencils, often work precisely because they take our conscious minds off our topic. Our thoughts simply wander, and, as we all know, when our thoughts wander our best ideas often spring to mind. So, to begin your freewriting you just need a pen and paper or, more probably, a computer and keyboard, and a willingness to start. You just require a chunk of time that you are happy to devote to a good cause. You need commitment and a sense of adventure.

Be confident. Try not to agonize about what you are writing. Don't fret about your spelling or punctuation or worry about the formal composition of your paragraphs or even if you have any paragraphs at all. Simply write or type continuously, with relish. I'll stop now, however, before you accuse me of freewriting and let you try a topic so you can experience the qualities of this essential first step. Feel free to procrastinate before you start. Just set an alarm clock for thirty minutes or so and make yourself comfortable in front of your computer or over your paper. Then enjoy the exercise below.

EXERCISE 1: Freewriting

1. Choose a topic you have been assigned recently or a topic from the list below that you know something about and follow my advice for freewriting.

2. Think about the topic.

3. Read up on it as much as is necessary, just as you would were you preparing to write an essay on it for an assignment. Give yourself a time limit, but forget it as you write. Don't stop to consider what to write or how best to write it once you get going. Don't stop writing or typing. Don't correct spelling mistakes or worry about punctuation. If you lose one train of thought, then simply follow yourself to the next one.

4. When your time limit expires or you grow too tired to continue, then stop. Put away what you have written, preferably without reading it straight away.

Sample Topics for Exercise 1

1. The advantages or disadvantages of social networking or of immigration control
2. The effects of economic downturns on the ambitions of young people
3. The best relationship between a nation and a religion
4. Individual, corporate, or government responsibility for negative outcomes from climate change
5. Glass ceilings for women or ethnic minorities
6. Competitive sport as a source of global unity or as a cause of unhealthy nationalism or tribalism
7. Rightness or wrongness of humanitarian intervention into the internal affairs of nations
8. Consequences of the emerging economic power of China and India on the developed Western nations
9. The effects – negative or positive – of the growing gap in individual wealth
10. The advantages of a university education that are not explicitly practical
11. The benefits or problems of having a comprehensive national health program
12. The belief that reality TV and celebrity culture determine public opinion more forcefully than politicians
13. The need to balance fun and enjoyment with hard work
14. A topic of your choice
15. A topic given to you by someone else (perhaps one of your lecturers)

STAGE 3

Mind Maps, Outlines, and Mapping Paragraphs
(With a Note of Caution)

After you have put your freewriting aside for a while, you will need to return to the first exercise and review closely what you have written. Most of the time, you will be pleasantly surprised by how much you have said. But, if you haven't accomplished much, don't despair. All you need from this stage is a paragraph, a line, or even a word that might form a basis upon which you might begin to formulate a response and move onto our next stage. If one doesn't seem there, reading through your ideas again might identify new ones, or you can take another stab at freewriting, perhaps after you have read more about your topic. Whatever you decide, once you have chosen ideas with which you can work, you will almost certainly want to organize them, however tentatively, and, for that reason, it's probably best always to follow the freewriting stage with a planning stage.

Mind Maps

One of the most common ways of organizing your freewriting is to create mind maps, also called spider grams/graphs or tree diagrams, roughly resembling a map or web through which some writers attempt to connect a range of related ideas. There are lots of effective ways of creating mind maps, but you may want to begin by circling an idea in what you have freewritten that strikes you as interesting or promising and that you think may provide a central concept of your essay. That idea can serve as the basis of your map. You may then look back at your freewriting and find other terms and ideas that relate to this idea and that you can attach to it in some manner. Just how you attach them – as linear branches or connecting circles – is a matter of choice, but it's likely that your initial freewriting may not be focused enough to provide many clear links. If not, however, you can, as I have said, try that stage again. Or you may find that your chosen idea helps you now to think of new terms, ideas, arguments, or concepts that you can link to it and to each other. But, in any case, do not worry if the ideas you first generate from your freewriting stage are not specific enough to create an extensive map, diagram, or tree. The mastermind stage that follows will help you to engender more.

A Sample Mind Map[6]

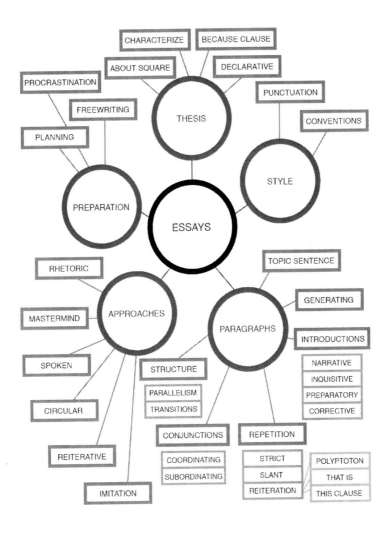

Outlines

Outlines are another method of essay preparation that some writers use. Like mind maps and diagrams, outlines allow you to identify potentially important ideas from your freewriting stage and to draw up provisional relations between and among them. In this way they can help you to begin to prioritize your ideas logically and symmetrically, organizing possible reasons that, you anticipate, may support and clarify your argument in the next drafting stage. Collecting your thoughts and aligning them in such a way should give you a better sense of the potential progression of your mastermind draft. It should allow you to state some idea of a provisional conclusion. In these ways, it may also increase your confidence before you move to the next stage of writing.

Examples of Outlines[7]

> ### Outline for an Essay about Lowering the Age Requirement for a Driver's License

1. *Introduction*
   a. Attention Getter
   b. Background Information
   c. Thesis Statement
2. *Supporting Point One*
   a. Support for Point One
   b. Evidence for Support
      i. Number of first time passers
      ii. Quote
      iii. Average time for driver's education classes
   c. Conclusion for Support of Point One
3. *Supporting Point Two*
   a. Support for Point Two
   b. Evidence for Supporting Point Two
      i. Number of students in post-test education
      ii. Quote
      iii. Number of students who do not commute by bus
   c. Conclusion for Support of Point Two

Outline for Essay about the Origins of Agriculture

1. *Agriculture Compared to Hunting-Gathering*
   a. Advantages of Agriculture
      i. More efficient use of land
      ii. Stable food source through the year
      iii. More free time in non-critical seasons
   b. Disadvantages of Agriculture
      i. Malnourishment
      ii. Labor intensive in critical seasons
      iii. High risk if crops fail
2. *Identifying Domesticates in Archaeological Record*
   a. Plants
      i. Seeds are bigger in size
      ii. Seeds' coats are thicker
      iii. Seeds found outside natural range of distribution
   b. Animals
      i. Horns change in morphology
      ii. Body size changes
      iii. Coat and fur change
      iv. Age-sex distributed in skeletal collections
      v. Species found outside natural range of distribution

Mapping Paragraphs

A third common method of planning is the mapping paragraph. Sometimes the first paragraphs of mastermind drafts, mapping paragraphs allow the writer to attempt to lay out the general direction of her essays, indicating what key topics she plans to explore or analyse in the body of the essays and sometimes even revealing the conclusions she intends to reach. In theory, mapping paragraphs not only provide opening guides that aid the writer, but they also alert the reader to the sequence and nature of the arguments he can expect to follow. Unlike mind maps or outlines, however, mapping paragraphs rarely set out supporting sub-topics. For this reason, you may find that they will work best for you as one part of a planning stage that also includes another form of planning such as a mind map or outline, and in our process we will always look to replace any mapping paragraph from our planning stage with one of the types of formal introductory paragraphs that we will discuss in Chapter 4.

Examples of Mapping Paragraphs

Example 1

This essay aims, in principle, to integrate historical developments with economic analysis to discuss the emergence of the First Industrial Revolution in Western Europe between the start of the seventeenth century and the end of the nineteenth century. It will do this by posing analytical questions in relation to three factors: the development and expansion of markets; the influence of the Enlightenment and scientific rationality; and the development and implementation of new technologies and the factory system. It will explore the economic impact of each of the factors and ask what conclusion we may draw from them.

> ## Example 2
>
> In this essay I will attempt to describe how the Second Industrial Revolution of the nineteenth century differed from the First Industrial Revolution of the late eighteenth and early nineteenth century. I will focus mainly on the roles played by science and technology and the special managerial challenges emerging in the operations of large firms. In order to achieve this aim I will briefly look at early stages of the First Industrial Revolution that had taken place in Britain within agriculture. I will include major factors that had contributed to increases in production and the commercialization of products. Furthermore I will look at other factors that were influenced by innovations and new systems and led to the Second Industrial Revolution. The economic and political systems of modern life have been greatly influenced by these factors.

You may use any of these three forms of planning or a combination of them to organize your thoughts after you have finished your freewriting stage. Or you may use another form if it works better for you. The key is to make some initial sense of your freewriting. But it is also vital that you observe a note of caution after finishing this stage. The best processes for writing argumentative essays encourage us – allow us – to be creative. They help us to give rise to ideas that we may not realize we have until we've articulated them.

As an essayist you should, therefore, try to remain as open as you can, for as long as you can, to those ideas that will almost inevitably occur to you as you write and revise your drafts. The act of writing is almost always the best breeding ground for good insights. The planning stage, in other words, does not in our process set out an order of ideas that you should then simply seek to translate onto the page when you write your mastermind drafts. Writing by outline or map, like painting by numbers, may work for a few. But professional writers, like professional painters, know it's most effective to combine planning with technique and inspiration. So don't be lulled into thinking that a mastermind draft based rotely on some form of planning stage will result in an effective final essay. A mastermind draft written to a plan will almost always, if not always, still arrive at a conclusion that differs from any one that you had originally set out. It will remain a mastermind *draft* that you will revise in subsequent stages of your writing process.

EXERCISE 2: The Planning Stage

1. Reread your freewriting exercise. Try not to worry if you've not written very much. It's only your first attempt, and sometimes your freewriting may conjure up little that seems immediately worthwhile. These things happen, and you'll have to be prepared to start again sometimes. (Indeed I hope you will return to the topics above and practice your freewriting exercise a number of times.) But my guess is that somewhere in what you have written you'll find some engaging ideas that are related to your topic. You may even have generated one potentially central idea you'll want to explore and develop, one you'll eventually want to convince your readers to accept. If you haven't, then you may need to research your topic more.

2. Whatever the case, now try to incorporate a planning stage into your process. Consider the relationships among your ideas and use them to write an outline, draw a mind map, or write a mapping paragraph (or do all three).

3. Repeat the freewriting exercise, starting with another topic. Then complete steps 1 and 2 again. Practice and repetition are crucial for the inexperienced writer. So be determined.

STAGE 4

The Mastermind Stage

Procrastination, freewriting, and some form of planning provide the first three stages in our writing process. Together they will aid you in the discovery of new ideas and points of view as well as new ways of arranging them. The mastermind stage that follows will enable you to generate more ideas at the same time as you initially incorporate them into a format that will eventually inform your final essay. As we have discussed, you will first often signal your central argument in the conclusion you reach in a mastermind draft, typically prefacing it with the words "In conclusion." This conclusion may follow from the plan that you have devised from your freewriting. If, as you should, you remain open to ideas while you write or type your mastermind draft, however, the conclusion at which you arrive may represent a genuine discovery. But, whatever conclusion you reach in your mastermind draft and however you reach it, it is vital that this draft does *not* mark the end of your process. Mastermind-style drafts are not the same thing as final argumentative essays. They represent only the fourth stage of our process, which we will follow with a fifth stage. Before we discuss that argumentative or persuasive stage, however, you need to create some text from the mastermind stage with which to work.

EXERCISE 3: The Mastermind Stage

1. Select one of the mapping paragraphs, outlines, or mind maps and diagrams that you have written for exercise.

2. From that paragraph or plan, write a mastermind draft of 1,500 or more words exploring your topic. Ideally, this draft will lead you to an expression near the end of what is or has become your main argument. You may precede its expression with the words "In conclusion," but, if not, you should still be able to identify what seems to be the central point of your concluding paragraph. Wherever it appears, however, do not worry about following your original intentions.

3. Do not worry about deviating from your plan or reaching a different conclusion. Just write a mastermind essay, with its typical linear structure (just don't submit it as such), and, after you have finished, identify as focused a statement of your overall conclusion as you can.

STAGE 5

The Argumentative or Persuasive Stage

The first step in our fifth stage is so simple it's almost embarrassing. You have practically completed it once you have made the decision not to stop at the end of the mastermind stage, not to submit your mastermind draft as if it were your final essay. As we learned in the Introduction, enacting this stage requires nothing more or less than physically copying and pasting your conclusion-as-thesis at the beginning of your mastermind draft to create a draft thesis. Doing so will not detract from the impact of your conclusion. Indeed, as you follow the instinctive structure of spoken rhetoric and make your essay circular and reiterative, its impact will more than double.

The second step in stage five requires more time and thought, however, for it represents the moment when you must first exchange your role as a writer for one as an objective reader. In this role, you should check to see where your ideas need further development. You should consider whether you need to re-arrange their order or provide clearer links between and among your supporting evidence and analysis. (You normally will, at least to some extent.) You should begin to assess your style and expression and evaluate the quality of your paragraphs. Whatever your observations, you should aim to ensure with your revisions that your reader will be able to follow your argument clearly and coherently from its expression as thesis to its reiteration as conclusion.

EXERCISE 4: Argumentative Stage: Cut, Paste, and Reflect

1. Go back to the mastermind draft that you wrote for exercise 3. Locate your conclusion and copy the sentence or sentences that express it most explicitly. Then paste that sentence or sentences at the start of your mastermind draft. (If you think your whole final paragraph represents your conclusion and you cannot paraphrase it, then copy and paste the entire paragraph. You will eventually have to refine it into an effective thesis. If you have written a mapping paragraph to begin your mastermind draft, delete it before you paste in your conclusion.)

2. Stop being a writer and read your essay carefully, as would an unbiased and constructively critical reader.

3. Reflect on the way in which reiterating the original conclusion at the start changes the structure of the draft and the experience of your reader.

4. Reflect also on the extent to which the content of your draft now relates to the opening statement of your conclusion and its final expression. (Does it seem to move from the general to the specific, for instance, and, if not, how might you shift some key ideas around so that it can?) Note any places where it seems as if a reader might lose the thread of your argument. Evaluate your paragraphs. Are they all complete enough to explain their central topic? We will discuss way of revising and improving your paragraphs in the next chapter.

SUMMARY

All good writers follow some type of process with their writing, and the process we have been building should be natural, straightforward, and easy to understand. It should rest on fairly familiar territory. Our active starting point involves freewriting, although I encourage you to precede this stage with your own style of productive procrastination and to follow it with a planning stage using mind maps, diagrams, outlines, and/or mapping paragraphs. We then follow these stages with our version of the ever-popular but deficient mastermind essay, mindful, however, that the best essayists always leave themselves open to inspiration and new ideas during this first act of composition. We promise, that is, to consider our mastermind essays as drafts and *not* as final essays. Instead, we agree to revise these drafts in subsequent stages before submitting our final essays. Our fifth stage of revision – our argumentative or persuasive stage – will finalize the steps, ensuring that we duplicate the *circular* and *reiterative* structure of spoken attempts at persuasion after we have exchanged our role as writer for one as reader. In the chapters that follow we will establish the next three stages. For now, however, I have set out the stages we have included so far so that you can remind yourself where our process is taking us.

Current Stages in Our Writing Process for Argumentative Essays

1. **The Procrastination Stage:** Once you have decided on your topic, you may find that you need to take your time to settle into the routine that characterizes the process you use for writing your essays. If so, there is no reason to worry. Just incorporate whatever form of procrastination, if any, puts you in the right frame of mind to begin writing, as long, that is, as that procrastination remains only a stage in your process.

2. **The Freewriting Stage:** When you are ready to start writing towards your essay, first set aside around 30 minutes and write with abandon about your topic. Do not stop to mull over what you have written or what you want to write. Do not worry about your structure or the

coherence of what you are writing. Just write and let your writing guide your thinking. Let your writing inspire you. Then take a break.

3. **The Planning Stage:** After your break, reread your freewriting to see if you can determine what key points you have made and which of them you want to pursue initially in your first draft. Before pursuing them, however, organize in some way the ideas that you have generated through your freewriting stage. You may choose to write an outline. Or you may prefer to devise a mind map or to write an opening paragraph mapping out your aims. Or you may decide to combine two or more of these. Whatever your choice during this stage, try not to become too attached to the shape and conclusion of your plan. Remain open to ideas that occur to you during the next stage and be prepared to go off plan as you write or type.

4. **The Mastermind Stage**: Compose a mastermind draft based on your freewriting and any planning you have done. Write or type yourself to a conclusion and identify that conclusion with the phrase "In conclusion," or whatever comes naturally to you. Resist the temptation, however, to think that you have now completed your assignment simply because you have written yourself to your word limit and your first conclusion. To help you resist, you may want to label this effort clearly as a "draft," for you still have more stages in your writing process.

5. **The Argumentative or Persuasive Stage**: Copy the conclusion at the end of your mastermind draft and paste it at the beginning. Ideally your mastermind conclusion will consist of one to three sentences at most. If not, see if you can rephrase any longer conclusion more concisely before copying and pasting it. If your mastermind stage has included a paragraph that maps out an original plan, simply delete it before pasting in your conclusion. If not, then paste the conclusion at the top of your draft. Then you will have re-structured your mastermind draft by making it *circular* and *reiterative*, as when constructing an argument in conversation. You will have established your second draft before swapping your role as a writer for one as an informed and conscientious reader.

CHAPTER 2

The Weighty Stage: Thesis Statements

> "Writing clear thesis statements upfront is hard
> work. That's why so few people write them."
> (Mark Tredinnick, *Writing Well: The Essential Guide*)[8]

Essay writing presents us with a series of paradoxes, one of
which is this: the harder an element or an activity may seem in
the abstract, the easier it often proves to execute in practice – and
vice versa. And probably no element of any argumentative essay
illustrates this paradox more than the thesis statement. As we
have seen, creating the first draft of our thesis statement involves
a simple act. We simply re-situate the conclusion that we express
in our mastermind draft, often prefaced either explicitly or
implicitly by the phrase "In conclusion," at the start of our draft.
Yet, for all of this initial ease, it is difficult, as Tredinnick
acknowledges, to write a good, truly effective thesis, one that
establishes your central argument succinctly. As a consequence,
it's usually necessary to continue to revise your thesis
throughout your process, even up to and at its end, which is
why we will devote an entire chapter to this key element of your
essays. Whatever your timing or strategy for revision, however,
before any of us can begin to revise the draft thesis statements
that we've copied and pasted in our argumentative stage, before
we can expect to write "clear thesis statements upfront," we
must have a sound understanding of the qualities that
characterize such statements.

What is a Thesis Statement?

A thesis statement is the concise, declarative sentence or
sentences that express the central argument of your essay.

What is the Purpose of a Thesis Statement?

The purpose of a thesis statement is twofold. First, it gives your readers a clear statement at the start of your essay of the view that you want them to accept as valid, at worst, and, at best, to be convinced of. Secondly, it establishes the *circular* and *reiterative* structure of your essay.

What are the Qualities of a Good Thesis Statement?

A Good Thesis Statement IS

1. Part of the **Opening of your essay**: it appears at the start of your essay, usually at the end of a formal introductory paragraph (the subject of Chapter 4) so that your readers know from the beginning what point you are going to argue and, as a consequence, can follow your argument more coherently as you provide supporting evidence.

2. **Declarative**: it is phrased as a declarative sentence rather than as a question. ("New York is the greatest city in the world" and not "Is New York the greatest city in the world?")

3. **Concise:** it states the central argument of the essay as directly as possible.

4. As **Specific** as possible: it avoids the language of the mapping paragraph. It does not, that is, just narrate what the writer intends to do in her essay. ("In this essay, I will do so and so. I will explain why such and such is as it is. I will conclude by considering whether the reason such and such is as it is right or wrong" does not form a thesis statement.)

5. **Subjective rather than objective**: it expresses the writer's opinion rather than a fact.

6. **Contestable**: it states an opinion that the writer assumes that his reader will not accept just because he expresses it. In other words, a thesis must be contentious, designed to need further justification, proof, or persuasion. It should not evoke immediate assent or agreement.

7. **Explanatory**: it at least implies a reason to support its contestable position. It hints at "why" a thesis is valid or true.

A Good Thesis Statement IS NOT

1. **Simply a Conclusion**: it does not merely repeat the writer's conclusion verbatim at the start of the essay, although, as we have said, a thesis can begin life as a draft conclusion. In fact, it is often good practice for a writer to reiterate her thesis as her conclusion since a circular and reiterative structure is very effective and comes naturally to us.

2. **Descriptive**: it does not describe what should follow or say that the writer will explain "how" his chosen topic is as it is.

3. **Factual**: it does not state a fact or a truism such as "Little Rock is the capital of Arkansas."

4. **Assertive**: it does not articulate an idea that the writer thinks the reader will accept at face value just because the writer states it.

5. **An Intention**: it does not simply indicate the theme of the essay nor express an intention with respect to what the writer will explore in a text or set of texts.

6. **Hidden**: it does not appear somewhere in the body of your essay as if it were the essay equivalent of a jack-in-the-box ready to pop up randomly in your essay.

Guides to Writing Good Thesis Statements

There is no magic formula for writing thesis statements. To write a truly effective thesis you must know the central argument of your essay extremely well, and no one can think for you. Moreover, each thesis will demand a slightly different tack or strategy, just as each essay dictates its own development, to some degree. There are, however, methods you can learn to help you revise your initial thesis statements and so make them as concise and influential as possible by the time you submit your final essays. These methods, as you will see, essentially involve applying a set of simple principles, asking yourself various questions about your thesis statements, and/or making vital substitutions as you explore ways to revise them. You may not apply all of these strategies all of the time. Sometimes you may not employ any of them, and, as you gain more experience, you may not even be aware if and when you are applying them. So don't take any of my advice as prescription. Writing thesis statements requires independence of thought. But creating a good final thesis necessitates a revision process every bit as crucial as the one for your essays overall.

'About Squared': Distinguishing Thesis Statements from Themes, Topics, and Issues

The essays that you write will often be in response to a question or statement that someone else, such as a university lecturer, has posed for you. Or they will require you to respond to a text or texts that you have read. In each instance, you will have to consider what we might call an issue, a theme, or a topic, synonyms that signify what your essay is mainly about. You may signal this 'about-ness' through your mind maps or outlines or in a mapping paragraph at the start of your mastermind stage. One essay, for example, may be about the developing climate crisis. Another may be about the digitalization of media or the ethical debates about the virtues of having a comprehensive health insurance program. Or you might discuss the theme of young love in Shakespeare's *Romeo and Juliet*. Similarly, you may focus on a central issue of George Orwell's essay "Politics and the English Language," and his claim that politics has contributed to the degeneration of the English language.

Although we don't need to examine the precise reasons here, the possibilities for what any text or set of texts is about are endless, in theory, as infinite as the number of possible readers of Orwell's essay or Shakespeare's play or the people considering climate change. The theme of *Romeo and Juliet*, for instance, might also be said to be "death" or "the dangers of disobeying parents" or "the deceptive nature of appearances." In spite of its writer's explicit claim, Orwell's essay might be "about" any issue or topic that any individual reader credibly infers from it. (Remember that readers infer ideas from texts; writers (or texts) imply ideas through their language and structure.) The point is that any text, regardless of discipline, can be said to be about almost anything.

It is therefore probably impossible to dispute someone's claim for a theme. A thesis, by contrast, expresses your opinion. It must be subjective and contentious, open to debate. It must incite argumentation and not aspire to immediate assent. In this way, a thesis tells your reader what your view is about your given theme. It articulates, in other words, what you want to argue about the theme or issue that establishes what your essay is about. Your thesis, that is, represents an 'about squared' (thesis $=$ about^2). It seems it is not only math that lets us play with square numbers.

"Specify, Specify, Specify": Making Your Thesis Statements as Focused as Possible

Issues, themes, and topics typically take the form of abstractions or general ideas. By contrast, the best thesis statements are concrete and specific. The more definite your thesis, the better it will serve your argument. Yet most inexperienced writers, including students who lack confidence in their writing, usually state their central arguments too imprecisely or evasively. As a result, their arguments remain vague or descriptive, partly because they worry about not having enough to say if, in their view, they define their topics too narrowly. So they try to protect themselves by setting out an overly general thesis. Yet, in one of the paradoxes of our process, not being specific enough represents the worst form of protection. It inevitably allows writers to waffle, to drift off the track of their arguments.

For that reason, always strive to express your central argument as precisely as you can. Remembering the following mantras will help you achieve this aim: "Specify, specify, specify." "Characterize, characterize, characterize." Using these guidelines will help you to examine and scrutinize the initial conclusion you have pasted as your draft thesis and begin to determine what ideas lie behind it, inform it. You can then revise the way in which you have written your draft thesis until you are pretty sure you can't specify or characterize it any more exactly without distorting it, until you think that you can't denote the crux of your argument any better or more succinctly. You will then have probably nailed your thesis. And you will have probably just nailed your essay as well.

Examples of Thesis Statements Expressed Too Abstractly

a) Chapter twenty-seven of *Wuthering Heights* is significant to understanding the rest of the novel.
b) Class remains the most pressing problem of social interaction.
c) The American dream has been fundamental to the development of American consciousness.

In each of the above examples we can identify at least one indefinite word or phrase that we can define more specifically. In example a) that word may be "understanding" or it may be "significant." In example b) it's "pressing" and in example c) "fundamental." Pinpointing precisely what we mean by these abstractions immediately helps us to refine our thesis, as I hope these revised examples will show.

a) Chapter twenty-seven of *Wuthering Heights* demonstrates that images of enclosure throughout the novel signify the irrational nature of Heathcliff's violence.

Now you may not know the text well enough to judge whether my specification of "significant to the rest of the novel" is accurate or potentially valid, but its validity is not the main point here. Instead the point is our attempt at characterization, our attempt to transform the abstract claim about the overall significance of the chapter to the novel into one that is more individual and debatable, one that will now give the essay a more exact focus.

b) Class remains the most intractable problem of social interaction.

I've given you a quick, possible solution, changing only one word from the first thesis attempt: "intractable" for "pressing." But isn't "intractable" more precise than "pressing"? Doesn't it characterize the problem and the issue at least slightly more individually? Ideally, however, you may want to define the idea of "social interaction" in more concrete terms as well. But I will leave that step for you to consider.

c) The American dream places individual responsibility at the center of American consciousness.

Here I have made a stab at distinguishing the "fundamental" relationship of the American dream and American consciousness, albeit in a fairly conventional way. I might, of course, have gone further in my characterizing zeal and defined for my readers the concept of the American dream itself. That way, I would have particularized our first abstract concept of "fundamental" even more.

"Why, Oh Why, Oh Why?" Questioning Your Way to More Succinct Thesis Statements

Another technique for revising your initial thesis statements is to ask yourself a series of questions about them until you are satisfied that they are as concise as possible. This process is similar to the one we will rely on later with paragraphs, and the aim is similar: to move from the general to the specific or from the least important to the most important. With thesis statements, however, the final aspiration is a single declarative sentence rather than a fully developed paragraph. For example, with the thesis statement above that claims "Class remains the most intractable problem of social interaction," we might initially ask ourselves why we have said economic conditions are so crucial to social interaction. Or, in a variation of the same process, we might ask why it is that class matters so much and what it is about class that affects people's interaction with others. We might ask further why its effect on social interaction is greater than other possible causes such as gender or ethnicity or geography. The crux is not necessarily what question or questions you ask, but whether the ones you ask put your first broad thesis under scrutiny. "Why?," "What?," "How?" are all productive.

Whatever questions you pose, the act of answering them needs to reveal what concrete ideas have backed up your more general ones. Each time you uncover a reason for your thesis, each time you demand further proof that you know your thesis well, you express it more clearly and directly. There is, of course, a limit to the number of times you can usefully ask yourself such questions, and you don't want to overdo it. Yet, if you don't scrutinize your thesis sufficiently, then rest assured your reader will scrutinize it for you, either consciously or unconsciously, as she reads. And she won't always answer your questions as you might have wished. More likely, she won't even bother answering them at all. So try not to forget: the more exact and opinionated your thesis is, the more focused your essay will be. The more focused your essay is, the more coherent it will be. And the more coherent your essay is, the more persuasive it will become.

Questioning Our Examples

> a) Chapter twenty-seven of *Wuthering Heights* demonstrates that images of enclosure throughout the novel signify the irrational nature of Heathcliff's violence.

Why does chapter twenty-seven confirm the influence of images of enclosure? How do these images affect the way the reader judges the nature of Heathcliff's violence?

> b) Class remains the most intractable problem behind social interaction.

Why might class remain so "intractable?" What characterizes its "intractable" nature? To what does "social interaction" refer precisely?

> c) The American dream places individual responsibility at the center of American consciousness.

Why is "individual responsibility" at the center of American consciousness? Why does its central role matter? What is the effect of that centrality? Why, why, why, why? Never grow tired of asking yourself "Why?" Or "How?" Or "What?"

The 'Because Clause' Step: Another Strategy for Revising Your Thesis Statements

When asking yourself questions about your thesis statements, it's entirely natural to leave the answers in your head, as it were. The danger of this tendency is, however, that the answers stay just there: in your head. One means of avoiding that problem is to include what I will refer to inelegantly as the 'because clause' step for your revision. As the name suggests, this step involves adding a dependent clause beginning with the subordinate conjunction *because* to your original draft thesis. Your draft thesis would then assume this temporary form: "My argument about my given topic is such and such because of so and so." Not only does this formulation force you to think carefully about the chief reason behind your thesis, but it also provides you with an explicit guide for the revision of the supporting argument in the body of your essay. You can then rewrite the 'because clause' draft that we have identified so that the final expression will display all of the characteristics of a succinct declarative thesis that we have identified.

a) Chapter twenty-seven of *Wuthering Heights* confirms the way in which images of enclosure throughout the novel signify the irrational nature of Heathcliff's violence *because* it dramatizes no good reason for Heathcliff's five-day imprisonment of Nelly Dean.

b) Class remains the most intractable problem behind social interaction *because* individuals find it harder to admit social and financial distinctions than they do differences of ethnicity and gender.

c) The American dream places individual responsibility regardless of circumstance at the center of American consciousness *because* it values personal aspiration above collective well-being.

As you can see, the 'because clause' represents an alternative starting point for the specific individualization of your final thesis. Yet you will want to refine this stage by removing the 'because clause,' as I have in the examples below, and then refining the expression of your final thesis.

a) As one of the repeated images of enclosure in *Wuthering Heights*, the five-day imprisonment of Nelly Dean in chapter twenty-seven confirms that the irrational nature of Heathcliff's violence cannot be curbed by love.

b) The difficulty individuals have admitting their economic status renders class the most intractable of all problems of social interaction including gender and ethnicity.

c) The American dream that everyone can succeed has left the ideal of personal aspiration before collective well-being at the center of American consciousness.

(You might, of course, want to refine these versions even further.)

"That" not "How": Being Declarative Rather Than Descriptive

Another common mistake novice writers make when they attempt to write a thesis centers on the use or misuse of the simple words *that* and *how*. Both words are subordinating conjunctions. Many experienced writers, however, rely more on the latter rather than the former, and the difference in effect is as crucial as it is subtle. Using "how" tempts us to describe our theme or text rather than arguing our thesis, although we probably won't be conscious of this temptation. For the natural reaction whenever anyone asks us "how" something works, "how" some writer argues what he argues, or "how" we get to some place or another is to give directions or to describe the actions or examples associated with our claim.

By contrast, substituting "that" immediately turns the thesis into a claim that needs to be explained and supported. It forces us to analyse our topics. If an essayist writes, for example, that a novel shows "that" its writer portrays women as more intuitive and practical than men, she will not only have to describe the respective characters, but she will also have to compare the respective portraits. She will have to argue the case for the writer's bias rather than leaving the reader to infer it. Making such a case, like arguing any thesis, will be more demanding than describing a group of actions or points or a cast of characters. If that were not the case, I doubt any of us would be inclined to rely on "how" in the first place. Such is the paradoxical nature of thesis statements.

To make sure that you give yourself the best chance of explaining "why" rather than describing "how," always double-check yourself when you phrase your thesis to include "how." It won't always be a mistake to use "how" rather than "that," and many of your final thesis statements will include neither subordinating conjunction. But at least try substituting "that" when your early drafts include "how." The substitution will probably reveal the ways in which you will want to develop a supporting explanation for your argument.

Examples of the Benefit of Using "That" Instead of "How"

a) The author explains how the American dream has been fundamental to the development of American consciousness.

vs.

The author explains *that* the American dream has been fundamental to the development of the American consciousness (because...)

b) George Orwell demonstrates how politics causes the degeneration of the English language.

vs.

George Orwell demonstrates *that* politics causes the degeneration of the English language (because...)

c) *Romeo and Juliet* shows how young love is destined to fail.

vs.

Romeo and Juliet shows *that* young love is destined to fail (because...)

Thesis Statements: Examples of Other Errors

Below are examples of other errors that inexperienced writers often make. Under each category, I have explained one example. Avoiding these mistakes will help you with the exercise that follows. As a preparation for that exercise, you might want to try to improve on the examples below once you have read my explanations. But accept our paradox: the process of writing effective thesis statements may seem ongoing and time-consuming. The time spent perfecting your thesis, however, will be time saved when you revise the content of your essays.

1. A Potentially Contentious Thesis Statement That Remains Too General

There is much in both *The Sound and the Fury* by William Faulkner and *Invisible Man* by Ralph Ellison to suggest that their protagonists inherit their plights.

This thesis statement contains a fair amount of potential. But I assume it is easy to spot the problem. What does the writer actually have in mind by the concept "much"? What characterizes this 'much-ness'? How exactly do these two novels by two of America's most provocative twentieth-century novelists suggest the inheritance of the respective plights of their protagonists? What about their inheritance does this 'much-ness' suggest? How does it suggest that both inherit their plights? What results from this inheritance?

The possible questions seem endless because the initial thesis is so vague. The writer might well have started with such an overarching statement as part of the opening of her mapping draft, continuing with sentences such as "In this essay I will examine the various elements in the novels that contribute to this suggestion. I will explore the consequences of this inheritance and compare them. I will conclude by considering what this fact tells us about something." But, at some stage, she will need to make her starting thesis more direct, more declarative, and more contentious: "The protagonists of *The Sound and the Fury* by William Faulkner and *Invisible Man* by Ralph Ellison both inherit their plights..." (Try suggesting now a step to make this thesis more exact.)

2. A Fact Passed Off as a Contentious Opinion

> The notion of alternative conceptual frameworks has been commonplace in our culture since Hegel.

This claim surely is either true or false. How can a reader think otherwise, given that the writer herself says the notion is "commonplace?" The only possible dispute would involve whether it has been commonplace since Hegel or before. Yet the more interesting question involves *why* the notion has been so commonplace. What is the reason behind its becoming commonplace? Or, we might ask, what it is about the notion that makes it commonplace. (What *defines* this notion, in other words?) For surely people must hold some difference of opinion concerning the reason behind its fate or what qualities most importantly determine that fate. Or you might ask yourself what results from this fact, what is the *consequence* of it. And, having asked ourselves these questions, we might then revise the thesis either by adding a 'because clause' or specifying the thesis more:

> The notion of alternative conceptual frameworks has been commonplace in our culture since Hegel *because* ...

OR

> The *something or other* about the notion of alternative conceptual frameworks has been commonplace in our culture since Hegel.

OR

> The *so and so* notion of alternative conceptual frameworks has been commonplace in our culture since Hegel.

All of these revisions provide a more exactly worded claim for us to argue. They transform a fact into an opinion that we assume our ideal readers will either dispute initially or not accept simply because we have said it. In other words, they change a truism into a possible thesis.

3. A Potential Thesis Statement Framed as a Question

Our working definition of a thesis statement should mean that you never make this all-too-common mistake. A question is obviously not a declarative sentence. Therefore you must *never* frame a thesis statement as a question. In fact, if anything, a thesis represents the answer to a question.

> Not "Why did Native Americans not demand more compensation for the island of Manhattan?" but "Native Americans did not demand more compensation for the island of Manhattan because. . ."

> Not "How far does the so-called frontier identity determine American narratives of self and nation?" but "The so-called frontier identity does such and such or so and so to the American narratives of self and nation."

4. An Unsupported Mapping Statement of Intention

> It is possible to see why the protest was significant by looking at the relationship of its central aims to the political context as a whole.

This statement would probably be more likely to appear as part of a mapping paragraph at the start of a mastermind essay. It's also something of a truism, for surely everyone would agree that it is theoretically likely that looking at a protest in a political context might reveal something significant. Think back, however: a good thesis moves beyond a truism to express an individual opinion. The writer should discover just what that significance is when she writes her mastermind draft. She can make sure she answers some if not all of these questions: Why is the protest significant? How would you characterize its significance? How would you define its relationship to the central objectives of the political context? What are these central objectives? She might try "The relationship of the central objectives of the political context demonstrates that the protest was significant because..." or "The relationship of the central objectives (the writer would want to name the objectives explicitly) shows that the protest does such and such within the political context as a whole."

EXERCISE 5: Submitting Your Thesis Statements to Scrutiny

1. In Exercise 4 you copied the conclusion of your mastermind draft and pasted it at the beginning of that draft. With that step you essentially created a thesis for your argumentative stage. (Remember: try to limit your relocated conclusion to no more than three sentences. Ideally it will consist of only one sentence.) Now refine your thesis by submitting it to any or all of the methods of scrutiny set out in Chapter 2. Your aim should be to rephrase your thesis as precisely and effectively as possible.

2. Compare your revised thesis with your original conclusion and consider whether you may also want to rephrase the latter so that the two work together to structure your draft as well as possible.

3. Reflect on how the expressions of your thesis and conclusion may affect a reader's perception of the relationships among the supporting ideas in the body of your draft. Consider any possible changes you may want to make to the order or development of your supporting ideas as a result of your revision.

4. Exchange the work you have completed for the first three steps with another writer or fellow student and provide constructive criticism for each other.

EXERCISE 5a: Thesis Statement Revisions

1. Below are twenty-five examples of draft thesis statements.

2. Consider which, if any, of them may represent thesis statements that you think do not need any further revision or that would be acceptable as a final thesis in an argumentative essay.

3. Revise all of the remaining examples, using some or all of the stages of revision we examined in Chapter 1.

Examples

1. The First and Second Industrial Revolutions have had significant influence on modern life.

2. This essay will explore the main themes of crime prevention using environmental controls whilst assessing the effectiveness and moral implications of using such methods.

3. The effect that different perceptions of beauty and vanity have on the behavior and emotions of the main character shows why she rejects the advances of her suitor.

4. Each of the three cultural theories challenges the conventional image of women by arguing how women should be even more free-thinking and decisive.

5. Although earlier detective films may be as stylish in their own ways as *The Maltese Falcon* is in its, what Huston's film adds to the genre is the dark side of human nature, the confrontation with irredeemable evil, and the determination of the hero to disclose the truth about the sordid experiences he has endured.

6. The economic and political systems of modern life have been greatly influenced by three main factors.

7. Does the treatment of death by psychologists from different countries reflect their respective cultural perspectives?

8. In *The Grapes of Wrath* John Steinbeck challenges the American myth that keeps selling a dream that is realistically unobtainable.

9. The film features elements of African-American culture, displaying a cross-section of various communities across the South and presenting characters of various ages and occupations.

10. Due to rising tuition fees, opposition to the expansion of higher education seems to be growing, and many see this as a step backwards as they believe it will create an enormous number of problems.

11. Oliver Stone resists the usual Hollywood format in which all the emphasis is rooted in the deeds of the hero rather than in an accurate representation of the experiences of war.

12. The values of self-reliance advocated by Ralph Waldo Emerson remain as alluring now as when he wrote them in the mid-nineteenth century, but are they at odds with our contemporary need for community-spirited action?
13. Financial deregulation is the main cause of the growing inequality of incomes.
14. The physical journey of the heroine and her relationship with residents at both houses serve as an allegory for unbalanced flux in the spiritual relationship between the two families.
15. Are the acquisition of knowledge and the understanding of new concepts that come through university life important from the standpoint of both the individual and society?
16. The emotions that the participants experienced during the experiment raise many significant issues for the whole culture.
17. The juxtaposition of deep inner psychological reflection and simple child-like response ensures that the key conflicts in the documentary convey real power and emotional intensity.
18. Although more diverse types of couples now entertain the possibility of marriage, divorce rates continue to rise.
19. The relationship between Mark Twain the author and Huck Finn the narrator must be seen as paternalistic.
20. By challenging the idealized femininity espoused by most Victorians, women novelists of the time promoted a psychological realism that is absent from their male contemporaries.
21. Both social theories explore the special needs of solitary people.
22. The central characters in the sitcom demonstrate how Americans no longer have equal access to the "American Dream."
23. The autobiography places the reader in a world where normality is inverted and the writer is forced to confront a world of contradiction.
24. More than anything else, a sense of isolation drives modern-day immigrants to take refuge in the world of their dreams.

25. The Industrial Revolution brought about the transformation of man from herdsman to manipulator of machines.

SUMMARY

Writing good thesis statements is hard. It requires a great deal of thought and a sufficient understanding of technique. As refinements of the most explicit statements of your relocated conclusions, good thesis statements must be as precise and well phrased as possible if they are to be truly effective. As a consequence, always make sure you leave enough time in your drafting process to revise your thesis statements as carefully as possible. You may even find it's a good idea to review your draft theses at each subsequent stage of your process, perhaps using a different combination of revision strategies as you proceed.

Current Stages in Our Writing Process for Argumentative Essays

1. **The Procrastination Stage:** Incorporate whatever form of procrastination puts you in the right frame of mind to begin writing.

2. **The Freewriting Stage:** Set aside around 30 minutes and write with abandon about your topic. Then take a break.

3. **The Planning Stage:** Reread your freewriting and then organize the ideas, trying not to become too attached to your plan.

4. **The Mastermind Stage**: Compose a mastermind draft, writing or typing yourself to a conclusion.

5. **The Argumentative or Persuasive Stage**: Copy the conclusion at the end of your mastermind draft and paste it at the beginning.

6. **The Weighty Stage – Thesis Statements:** Revise your newly pasted conclusion into a more effective thesis, using any or all

of the methods we have discussed. (These will differ depending on the length of conclusion you have originally copied and pasted. As you gain experience, try to copy and paste only the one or two key final sentences of your initial mastermind draft conclusion.) Think carefully about the best expression for your thesis. Writing a really good thesis requires quite a lot of hard thinking, not only about the precise nature of your main argument, but also the best way to express it. For this reason, it is always best to continue to revise your thesis, once after reading your argumentative essay for the first time during the Argumentative Stage and at least once again after you have made changes to the paragraphs that comprise the body of your essay in the Content Stage on paragraphs that follow.

CHAPTER 3

The Content Stage: Paragraphing, Argument, and Audience

> "The paragraph has a dual character: it is an essay in miniature, endowed with some measure of individuality, composed of related material, and as carefully designed as the essay itself; but it is also an integral part of the composition in which it stands."
>
> (Robin S. Harris and Robert L. McDougall, *The Undergraduate Essay*)[9]

The Content Stage is designed to help you draw out the specific ideas that support the argument informing your mastermind draft. These specific ideas almost always remain under-developed in that first draft. Yet you will need to express them fully and methodically if you expect to convince your readers of their validity. For a good essayist always considers (and respects) the opinions and assumptions of his readers. He does not try to convince a skeptical audience simply by shouting at them, so to speak, and, in many successful argumentative essays, the writer may even indicate where apparently opposing ideas are valid, or might be. But, even if he doesn't, he will at least show an understanding of those ideas. (Concession is almost always a good rhetorical ploy.)

So always strive to *argue* an opinion in your essays. At the same time, however, when you first read your argumentative draft, make sure that you do not depend on an argumentative tone for persuasion. Check your tone and your register while you consider the order of your argument, your supporting evidence that comprises the body of your draft, and make your revisions. To keep matters simple, let's say for now that it's almost always best to order that evidence from the least important ideas to the most important ones or from the most general to the most specific or, in exceptional cases, the other way around (from the most specific to the most general). And one of the best ways to learn the most effective structures for your essays and to apply that learning to your writing is to begin to pay more attention to the essays that you read. In theory, another way would be to adopt the method described by Stevenson at the opening of our introductory chapter and to imitate the essays of professional writers.

Imitating whole essays, of course, isn't very practical. But we can do the next best thing. We can imitate successfully structured paragraphs. As Harris and McDougall say above, paragraphs represent something like essays writ small. Many of the qualities that make argumentative essays coherent and persuasive, in other words, also make paragraphs coherent and persuasive. Yet paragraphs are much easier to imitate. And, in imitating good examples written by experienced writers, you can also "ape" a range of styles. Moreover, by paying close attention to the content of the paragraphs as you read them, you can learn a lot about a great many interesting subjects while picking up key pointers about structuring your essays. Imitating paragraphs of successful writers, that is, can enhance your understanding of the world – and that wider understanding is no small advantage for an essayist.

So, as you imitate the examples of good practice in the exercise that follows at the end of this chapter, consider how each paragraph develops. Think how each idea and sentence relates to the ones before and those that follow. Ask yourself why each paragraph works so you can later apply its techniques in your essays. Knowing what qualities you are aiming for as you revise your argumentative drafts will be vital. That knowledge will ensure that you develop and specify your ideas as you order them constructively. You will be able then to write effective paragraphs, and, when you can, you can also write effective essays. It's as simple – or as difficult – as that. Before you attempt any imitations, however, first have a look at the two samples below.

The Paragraph as an Essay Writ Small

Below are two paragraphs that seem to illustrate this point, standing as they do virtually as mini-essays in their own right, complete with formal introduction, thesis, supporting body of evidence, and reiterating conclusion.

Paragraph-Essay 1

Some people dislike the word *argument* because it sounds too pugnacious. But it is a civilized term; we make arguments instead of war. We persuade people rather than beat them into submission. Democracy depends on argument. Candidates argue that they are more qualified than their opponents; representatives argue that their policies are better than the alternatives. Lawyers and judges argue about what the laws mean. Citizens argue with each other about what's right or wrong with society. In tyrannies, people don't argue – at least not in public. Democracy is unending disputation.[10]

Paragraph-Essay 1: Annotated

"Some people dislike the word *argument* because it sounds too pugnacious. But it is a civilized term; we make arguments instead of war. We persuade people rather than beat them into submission."

(*The first sentences serve as a formal introduction, setting out an accepted opinion in order for the writer to refute it. Notice the use of "But" as a transitional device as well as the use of reiteration in the third sentence to reinforce and explain the point of sentence two.*)

"Democracy depends on argument."

(*Here is the thesis statement.*)

"Candidates argue that they are more qualified than their opponents; representatives argue that their policies are better than the alternatives. Lawyers and judges argue about what the laws mean. Citizens argue with each other about what's right or wrong with society. In tyrannies, people don't argue – at least not in public."

(These sentences develop an argument in support of the thesis statement by supplying the examples leading to a comparison.)

"Democracy is unending disputation."

(The last sentence expresses the conclusion, which reiterates the thesis, thereby creating a circular and reiterative structure, the link between the thesis and conclusion made stronger through the use of a synonym: "disputation" for "argument.")

Paragraph-Essay 2

The great misfortune of the modern English is not at all that they are more boastful than other people (they are not). It is that they are boastful about those particular things which nobody can boast of without losing them. A Frenchman can be proud of being bold and logical and still remain bold and logical. A German can be proud of being reflective and orderly and still remain reflective and orderly. But an Englishman cannot be proud of being simple and direct and still remain simple and direct. In the matter of these strange virtues, to know them is to lose them. A man may be conscious of being heroic or conscious of being divine, but he cannot be conscious of being unconscious.[11]

Paragraph-Essay 2: Annotated

"The great misfortune of the modern English is not at all that they are more boastful than other people (they are not). It is that they are boastful about those particular things which nobody can boast of without losing them."

(The first two sentences act as a formal introduction that corrects a mistaken view and states the thesis of the paragraph/essay.)

"A Frenchman can be proud of being bold and logical and still remain bold and logical. A German can be proud of being reflective and orderly and still remain reflective and orderly. But an Englishman cannot be proud of being simple and direct and still remain simple and direct."

(These sentences provide the body of evidence in the form of examples supporting the thesis. Note the way that the writer aligns the three sentences by using a similar sentence structure in all of them.)

"In the matter of these strange virtues, to know them is to lose them."

(This sentence reinforces the original thesis.)

"A man may be conscious of being heroic or conscious of being divine, but he cannot be conscious of being unconscious."

(Final sentence makes the paragraph circular and reiterative by rephrasing the thesis as conclusion.)

Topic Sentence Paragraphs

Paragraphs are something of a modern invention. Their beginning generally coincided with the proliferation of printed materials in the late eighteenth and early nineteenth centuries. Before then, writers regularly conveyed their ideas in continuous lines sometimes running to pages. They didn't use the form of indentation that – along with extra spaces for unindented groups of sentences – distinguishes one paragraph from another in most of the texts we read. We all know just how difficult it can be to read such a large body of prose, however, and writers, printers, and readers subsequently began to alleviate this problem. They developed the conventions of separation and indentation that characterize the cluster of sentences to which we now give the name "paragraph."

Modern paragraphs usually contain between three and ten sentences, although the length depends largely on the genre of writing. It's not uncommon these days, for instance, to read single-sentence paragraphs in some newspapers and novels. By contrast, you may find paragraphs extending beyond ten sentences in some academic monographs and journals or collections of essays. Whatever the length, however, and whatever the genre, by common agreement a paragraph typically consists of a group of sentences that explains a single topic or develops from an initial idea. Ideally a writer should know each topic or idea as well as she understands the central argument of her essay.

Contemporary convention used to require writers to state the central idea of their paragraphs in each paragraph's first sentence, and many textbooks continue to insist on following this tradition. That first sentence, the most important sentence in this type of paragraph, is called the *topic sentence*, the role of which is to establish the central focus of each paragraph. The obligation of each subsequent sentence is to explain, de-limit, or exemplify this central topic. As the example below demonstrates, each of these subsequent sentences thus assumes a similarly supporting or subservient relationship to the topic sentence and usually a relationship of the same type. Paragraphs built upon this *topic sentence model* therefore imply the shape of something abstractly resembling a wide-based pyramid, all subsequent sentences referring to the first topic sentence in the same way as if they were all aligned on the same plane in our imagination rather than in consecutive order.

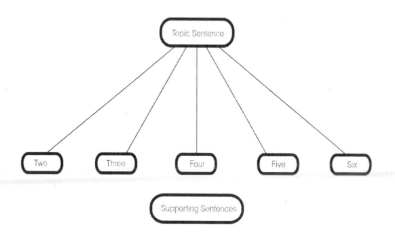

Here is a simple example of a topic sentence paragraph, which I have slightly revised to amplify a few points. The subject is *The Dean's December*, a novel by the American writer Saul Bellow, a Nobel Prize winner for Literature:

On a personal level, there is the same dispossession. Valeria, for example, has lost her early political hopes, her government job, her standing in society, her husband, her daughter, and now her ability to speak or to move; finally she confronts, with full awareness, the loss of her life. Minna is about to lose her mother, Gigi her sister. Back in Chicago, Ricky Lester has lost his life and his wife her husband. Even Dewey Spangler, following surgery, is forced to take a forward look to his own dissolution and Corde's cousin, Max Detillion, is moving down the same track, facing "neither virus nor bacteria, but erotic collapse." (71) In addition, Dewey makes Corde aware of his own accumulated losses: the early promise only partly fulfilled, the brilliant career he might have had. Even the Chicago in which they grew up has vanished under the polished grandeur of the present, and the youthful Dewey has also gone: "since then each of them had died at least three or four times." (122)[12]

The above paragraph exhibits perhaps the easiest strategy for developing a topic sentence paragraph. The first, or topic, sentence establishes the main idea of the paragraph: the occurrence of dispossession on a personal level. The sentences that follow help to justify this claim both individually and collectively by listing individual instances of loss. Valeria, Minna, Gigi, Ricky Lester, Dewey Spangler, and Max Detillion all lose something. All are dispossessed in some way. Each sentence that lists one of these dispossessions thus relates to the initial topic sentence in exactly the same way.

We may assume that the writer, in this case Martin Corner, has ordered the sequence of his examples according to some principle – let's say from the least to the most important type of loss since this order would be typical and effective. But, without knowing the novel well enough to say for sure, we could re-arrange these examples in any order without disturbing the sense of the paragraph's main idea. All of the sentences would maintain the same relationship to the topic sentence as they had before. They would all be similarly subordinate to it. Collectively they would help to transform the topic claim of the paragraph from a simple assertion into a well-supported, persuasive claim (comparable to the type of persuasive claim we need in our argumentative essays).

There are, of course, other types of development available to the writer of topic sentence paragraphs. She may, for example, compare and contrast her topic ideas. She may develop a cause and effect relationship. But, whatever the strategy, a writer using the topic sentence model ought to attempt to guarantee that each paragraph provides a clear and explicit focus that will allow her reader to follow her argument step by step throughout the essay. In fact, if you use the topic sentence model exclusively throughout your essay, your reader ought to be able to strip away each set of supporting sentences and understand the gist of what you are arguing in the essay as a whole simply by reading each topic sentence in turn. The skeleton of the argument could, in some respects, stand alone adequately without the flesh and blood of its development. It is probably for this reason that some lecturers may continue to ask you to start every paragraph in your essays with a topic sentence. Some may even require it.

If that's not the case, then you can be more flexible with the basic shape of your topic sentence model, as in this second example, written by a former student of mine at Kingston University on an early twentieth-century American novel.

In Willa Cather's novel *My Antonia,* readers can only speculate on the reasons that Jim does not marry Antonia. Jim may refuse to marry a socially and sexually disgraced woman, or he may desire to pursue a successful career. Or he may simply fear sex and sexuality. But one crucial reason seems clear. Jim does not choose to marry his childhood friend because he refuses to grow up and to face the complexities of adult life: "I wished I could be a little boy again," he tells Antonia. He longs to keep Antonia insulated from time and reality by creating the perfect image of her in his mind, even if maintaining that image means leaving her to her hardships with an empty promise to return soon.

As in the earlier example, this paragraph begins with a clear, declarative, thesis-like statement to announce the apparent topic: "In Willa Cather's novel *My Antonia* readers can only speculate on the reasons that Jim does not marry Antonia." (Jim is one of the main characters of the novel. Antonia is, as you might guess from the title, the protagonist.) The next two sentences follow the same pattern as before. They list three individual examples or reasons to back up the claim made in the first sentence. Some readers may think that Jim fails to marry Antonia because he considers her socially and sexually disgraced. Others may believe he refuses the chance for the sake of his career, still others that Jim fears sex and sexuality. Here again, the writer does not explicitly prioritize these three possible reasons for Jim's reluctance. She simply lists them as evidence of her knowledge of past debates about the novel and as equally valid – or invalid – interpretations of what must be a crucial moment in the narrative. Each reason, therefore, stands in precisely the same relationship to the first sentence as the other two, and up to this point the structure of the paragraph conforms to the classic topic-sentence shape.

The writer changes this shape tellingly, however, with the next sentence: "But one crucial reason seems clear." Here, rather than another example of a potential explanation for Jim's refusal, the writer now offers us something like a rebuttal. This alternative interpretation, she implies, differs in weight and significance from the other three by emphatically offering its own authoritative, counter-thesis-like claim. Furthermore, when the writer then defines that general claim more specifically – "Jim does not choose to marry his childhood friend because he refuses to grow up and to face the complexities of adult life"– the pyramid of her paragraph suddenly seems to have grown another apex. Her paragraph seems to have sprouted a second topic, this time expressed in two sentences that relate to the first one in a very different way from the two that preceded them.

We might say that the writer simply thinks that she needs to provide us with fewer examples to illustrate her point than the earlier paragraph, and that, had she extended her list of ideas, the sentence starting with "But" would have provided the topic sentence for paragraph two. And we might be right. Yet, as a result of her decision, the paragraph now provides a sense of development and progression rather than accumulation.

Suddenly readers feel as if we are in the midst of a process of thinking and argument rather than mere confirmation, and this process of thinking, of development, of active *persuasion*, continues until the end of the paragraph. First, the writer supplies a supporting quotation from the novel to provide authority to the claim about Jim's refusal to mature, just as you will sometimes provide quotations from the text you are analyzing or from a secondary source of information. She then completes the paragraph with a sentence that, in effect, explains just what she has meant by the preceding claim about Jim's lack of acceptance of "the complexities of adult life": "He [Jim] longs to keep Antonia insulated from time and reality by creating the perfect image of her in his mind, even if maintaining that image means leaving her to her hardships with an empty promise to return soon."

This explanation does more, however, than simply restate the earlier claim regarding Jim's rejection of life's complexities. It also clarifies the reason behind that rejection by expressing exactly what the writer thinks such "complexities" entail, which is the need to confront the effects of "time and reality," to let go of idealized images from the past: in this case, "the perfect image of her [Antonia that Jim clings to] in his mind." With this final sentence, the student accepts the obligation to state precisely what she means by her abstract concept, which here expresses the notion of "complexities," just as she did previously when she defined the "crucial reason" that refuted those commonly held by previous readers. This acceptance crucially distinguishes all good practice. Without it, the reader would be left to supply his own definitions. By giving hers, the writer, by contrast, directs her audience to the opinion she wants them to accept, towards the argument of which she hopes to persuade them, replacing general assertion with concrete, methodical explanation, which always represents a more successful tack.

In completing this rhetorical strategy, the last sentence in the paragraph does more than just duplicate the relationship of the previous sentence to the rest of the paragraph. It details that relationship, uncovering degrees of abstraction and argument which would have left the evidence of her claims much fuzzier and less convincing and at the mercy of her readers' interpretations were this sentence not in the paragraph. Repeating yourself in this way in your paragraphs and your essays, using rhetorical tools of *reiteration,* is not only effective, but also surprisingly straightforward and easy to do, as we saw in our sample paragraphs/essays.

Generating Model of Paragraphs

The above example shows us just how we can adapt and develop the classic model of the topic sentence paragraph. For this reason the best contemporary teachers of writing have increasingly appreciated that they need to offer less dogmatic advice to students. They have allowed, if not always encouraged, alternative models. They have accepted that topic sentences may, in some instances, appear elsewhere in the paragraph and that even very good writers sometimes use paragraphs that don't contain a conventional topic sentence at all. Indeed, at times, established writers legitimately choose only to imply a topic across the entire length of their paragraphs or across more than one paragraph. Sentences in such paragraphs relate as much, if not more, to the sentences that precede them and those that follow as they do to the first sentence in the paragraph. As a consequence, the abstract structure implied by these paragraphs suggests a shape that is less like a pyramid and more like a tower, each sentence developing the ideas of the preceding one before being developed in turn by sentences that follow, as the diagram and sample paragraph below both illustrate.

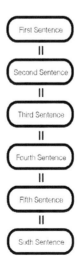

The following, slightly revised paragraph exemplifies this paragraph shape. It comes from one of the key books by the late influential American economist John Kenneth Galbraith. The paragraph argues for the wholesale effect of the economic downturn of the 1930s. As you read it, consider how the shape of its development compares with the earlier examples.

[Everything] changed very much during the decade of the thirties. The Great Depression brought production to a very low level. Between 1929 and 1933 the gross output of the private economy dropped by between a third and a half. The sheer magnitude of this movement focused attention, as never before, on movements in the total output of the economy and on their far-reaching consequences for economic and political fortune. Characteristically, to increase production was less central to men's thoughts than to reduce unemployment. "Our primary task is to put people back to work," [American President Franklin D.] Roosevelt said in his first inaugural. But whether directly or as a by-product of the effort to reduce economic insecurity, expanded production began to acquire a growing significance to political liberalism in its American sense.[13]

Much like the paragraph about Cather's novel, Galbraith's paragraph initially suggests the same implied shape as our first example of a conventional-topic-sentence paragraph. Its first sentence – "Everything changed very much during the decade of the thirties." – declares a potential topic for the entire paragraph. All of the sentences that follow, we assume, will help to tell us just what that "Everything" refers to and how it all changed. But, as with the paragraph on Cather, the sentences that follow relate to the first one in a different way. Indeed, even more so than in that previous example, each sentence builds upon and extends the idea from the preceding sentence more than it serves the opening one.

It's as if one big idea leads Galbraith to his next one, as if he's molding each sentence from parts of the clay of the previous one, taking a bit from the core, as it were, and then constructing a fuller idea from that smaller bit. Whereas the topic sentence model might be said to resemble a set of Russian dolls, each sentence replicating exactly the one before it, if on a smaller scale, as in the first example on Bellow, Galbraith presents us with a paragraph equivalent of a genealogical line, a family tree, each sentence springing as if from the same origin and thus bearing some resemblance to previous sentences. But each sentence is also crucially its own person, so to speak, adding its own individual qualities to the family traits. Each 'offspring' thus adds a sharper amount of detail – more specificity – to the paragraph's original design.

The 'progeny' that is the second sentence might not surprise us, as it cites an example of one change from the thirties: very low production. But the third sentence does not then list a second, similar example of change. It breaks the direct connection to the opening sentence of the paragraph, explaining the second claim about production levels: these levels dropped "between a third and a half." The fourth sentence alters this pattern of development still further, setting out the effect of the decrease rather than providing another evidence of change. The fifth sentence then expands on the new focus in sentence four on the nation's "attention" to "increase[d] production." Sentence six substantiates this point with a direct quotation, giving Galbraith's argument the benefit of what seems an authoritative voice, just as a similar move did in the example about Cather's novel.

Galbraith completes his paragraph by drawing a conclusion: "expanded production began to acquire a growing significance to political liberalism in its American sense." Yet his conclusion now seems far removed from his opening sentence, which we might have thought was designed to supply the paragraph's central topic. Galbraith has stuck to his topic, only in a different fashion. He's moved it along, not so much substantiating an existing foundation for that topic, as he might have done with a traditional topic sentence paragraph, but *generating* successive ideas from it throughout the length of his paragraph (just as you can when freewriting or writing your mastermind drafts).

This model, which is often referred to as the *generating model*, thus differs from the model devoted to topic sentences in at least one crucial way. It encourages us to think in the act of writing, either as part of our drafting stages or, just as likely in our process, when we revise. Writing a generating paragraph, that is, allows us to combine the activities of freewriting with revisions of our mastermind drafts, engendering new ideas and, importantly, supplying the clarifying specifics that will make our topics clearer and more persuasive. By contrast, worrying too much initially about starting each paragraph with a topic sentence as you write may scupper the flow of thoughts that create your mastermind drafts, much like sticking too rigidly to your outlines or mind maps, and it rests on the same mistaken premise: that we know before we write what it is we want to write, that we understand our argument before we explore it. An active process of writing, on the other hand, allows you to bring the acquisition and expression of knowledge into the present. You don't just recite views that you already realize that you know. Instead, you actively discover new ideas or uncover the specific foundations and the reasons for the general ideas you vaguely hold.

This act of discovery continues into your Content Stage. Just how you approach this stage, and what you will be looking for as you revise your argumentative stage drafts, will depend somewhat on the type of paragraphs you prefer to write. Revising topic sentence paragraphs usually centers mainly on the topic sentence itself. If you remain open to ideas as you write, you'll often find that you won't always have written appropriate topic sentences during the mastermind stage of your process. Indeed, you would almost certainly not be generating ideas effectively if you did. You will, by contrast, only discover what the topic of many of your paragraphs is as you revise, once you've transformed yourself into a reader and an editor. You may then want either to rewrite some or all of your topic sentences or, more likely, to add topic sentences to your existing paragraphs once you have determined precisely what the topic of the respective paragraph is. Only at such a point can we express clearly the opening sentences that set out the topics that our paragraphs explain.

The Content Stage with generating paragraphs is slightly different since our first sentences do not have to have the same comprehensive relationship to the sentences that follow. Nor do we have to be concerned about internal revisions taking us in a different direction from previous ones and thus destroying the pyramid shape of our paragraphs. Revising a generating paragraph thus allows us a more active, thorough, and helpful process of change. It also provides us with a great model for revision as a rule, for, when we edit and revise generating paragraphs, we must assess each individual sentence. We must check to see if we have explained each idea sufficiently well, if we have provided enough clarity and detail to our general assertions and claims. In other words, we must ask ourselves whether we have simply asserted some of our views, relying on skeptical readers accepting our claim, or whether we need to provide them with more concrete evidence and support.

The Length of Your Paragraphs

Incorporating the Content Stage will guarantee that you express yourself as methodically and completely as possible so that your readers will not only be able to understand the basis of your arguments but also be convinced by them. This strategy also goes to the heart of a second problem of most inexperienced writers: the length of their paragraphs. While there will be times when a one-sentence paragraph may be appropriate for writers, the majority of us write paragraphs that are too short. The reason for this problem may lie partly with newspapers and novels, both of which are sometimes typeset in very short paragraphs, presumably on the premise that most of us now have the attention span of a small child. Yet, whatever the reason, most students typically write paragraphs of three or four sentences at the most. Their ideas may be good and potentially convincing, but readers remain unpersuaded because they can't possibly know why, on so little evidence or explanation, they should believe something they may have previously rejected. The only readers likely to accept what we assert are those who already agree with us.

You may, by contrast, regularly write paragraphs that are longer than two or three sentences, paragraphs that are typically as long as the examples we have looked at, if not longer. You may find, however, that you have trouble translating that ability into one that allows you to string your longer paragraphs together to form a coherent essay. If you do, then you may not be writing fully developed paragraphs but rather just refusing to indent between assertions that lack sufficient support and which could probably provide topic or initial sentences for a series of separate paragraphs. Each of the sentences in your long paragraphs may remain overly general and poorly related to each other. Yet, since you should now have an idea about a process for generating effective paragraphs from short ones, you will be able to see that you are only facing the same problem from a different starting point. Therefore, you simply need to explain each sentence more fully and specifically, this time perhaps in separate paragraphs.

Whatever the current state of your paragraphs, however, short or long, it's likely that you are not developing your ideas fully. Our Content Stage can help you to correct this problem. And, once you understand its principles and learn a few of its techniques, you will find writing a greater source of inspiration and discovery as well as an exploration. Your essays will improve, and you will derive more pleasure from revising them more (and receive better responses). But the first step lies squarely with you. You must believe that your ideas are valid and rest on a potentially firm basis. You must also be willing to devote the time to construct these foundations, patiently and meticulously drafting your argument and your revisions. Ninety-nine times out of a hundred, the reason for our brevity is not a lack of ideas or stupidity, though I suppose we must concede that at times all of us may be accused of both (and maybe rightly). We all sometimes lack the knowledge we need to be persuasive. The main reason for our brevity, however, is usually either laziness or the failure to recognize what is required of us if we want to make our ideas clear enough for others.

Notice that I say *"failure* to recognize" here and not *inability* to do so, for anyone can learn how to determine what concrete ideas lie behind her broad statements and how to convey those ideas more specifically. More than thirty years of reading essays by developing writers has demonstrated to me that it is virtually impossible for any of us to make a statement that is completely unfounded. It's almost impossible to write a sentence, that is, that does not depend on some process of thinking that does not contain some more specific thoughts within it ('behind' it). All we need to do to uncover them is to ask ourselves the right questions, to share with our readers those exact reasons that allow us to express our sentence in the first place.

This simple process requires you to think in reverse, as it were, to identify those specific ideas that must inform your more general ones. These specific thoughts represent the evidence that you believe makes your idea valid, but that you have not put down on paper in your mastermind draft. Imagine your general idea as a ball of tangled wool, the sort for knitting or the type with which cats have a reputation for playing. As the knitter goes about his task, this bundle of tangled wool slowly takes shape between his needles. An object now seemingly inherent in the ball of wool emerges. That single, confused ball becomes transformed into a jumper or a scarf or pair of baby's mittens, the shape of which had existed within the tangle, waiting to be realized. The same process applies to your general ideas: as you uncover thoughts to explain these views, you slowly but surely transform them into the topics of your paragraphs. Their latent shape becomes apparent. You discover what it is you think, and, at the same time, you allow your readers to follow you more easily and clearly from start to finish, enjoying your paragraph or essay equivalent of a jumper, mittens, or scarf as they do.

Structure: Paragraphs as Guides to Essays

Before we look closely at ways of helping you turn your balls of wool into recognizable objects, however, let me say something about the structure of your essays as a whole. There are a number of classic ways of structuring a persuasive argument, including those we have indicated: general to specific, specific to general, and least important to most important. As with all elements in rhetoric, these structures have been identified from existing examples of good practice rather than presented as a theory or principle before the event. If you study these structures and practice them, you will find ways of relating them to the structure of individual paragraphs.[14] Adopting any of these strategies is infinitely better than developing ideas randomly, following one relatively important idea at the start of your paragraph, for example, with a much less relevant idea that, in turn, precedes your most crucial idea that is then succeeded by another reasonably insignificant idea, and so on. You get the picture.

Whatever your choice, when you revise your mastermind draft, you should aim to take your reader along a consistent direction as do the examples above. You should try to identify all of the abstract or unsupported claims that need to be explained and provide supporting evidence that has led you to make each one in the first place. In other words, you need to specify those claims, explain them. Specifying them may mean offering examples as in the first paragraph we looked at. Or it may mean substantiating a claim with a direct quotation, as in the second two examples above. It may even require you to define an abstract concept, since one way of uncovering your ideas is, as with thesis statements, to identify any unspecified phrases or ideas and explain them in more detail, characterizing them point by point.

Whatever pattern you choose, your mantra as reader and editor must again be "Specify, specify, specify." You must remind yourself to "Characterize, characterize, characterize" and "Explain, explain, explain," asking yourself "Why?" after each claim, as with thesis statements. Why is what you say accurate or true? Why should your reader accept it or believe it? Keep asking yourself such questions until either it no longer makes sense to continue to ask them or until you have satisfied yourself that the answer is as clear and precise as you can make it. For now, though, before we move to our examples of good paragraphs for you to imitate, let's work through two examples of improvable paragraphs.

Examples for Improving Paragraphs

Example 1

> Large classes can affect the learning of children. More will have to be invested to affect large classes.

Example 2

> The number of students benefiting from higher education in the UK has risen dramatically during the last decade and now stands at nearly 50%. The reasons behind this rise in further education are both political and social, but the question on most people's lips today concerns who will pay the tuition fees. Important and exciting changes are occurring but the question of finance should not blind us to these opportunities. Everyone has the right to achieve their (sic) potential through education irrespective of cost. As Aristotle said, "Educated men are as much superior to uneducated men as the living are to the dead."

Now let's read the examples again, starting with the first one.

Example 1

> Large classes can affect the learning of children. More will have to be invested to affect large classes.

In this example, the writer has left too much to the reader's imagination. Two sentences are seldom enough to make a good paragraph. For instance, how, exactly, do large classes affect the learning of children? What specific effects occur? Why do they occur? The writer should provide such details to back up his claim. If he were to accept his obligation and stop to ask himself just what lies behind his assertion, then he would be able to set out examples of the kind of effects he has in mind. But I'd wager that he could provide even more than that.

In the second sentence, we are entitled to wonder as readers what the writer means by the idea of "More." "More of what?," we might ask. We may assume he means more money, but he might have other ideas in mind. Let's say the latter, but to avoid confusion it might still help to specify areas on which extra money would be better spent. We may accept that he means that investing more money will result in a reduction in class sizes, for example. But, whatever our hunches, we can only guess what exactly he has in mind, and, in order to be convinced of his argument, we need to know what, for him, might be the precise consequences of this investment, what encouraged him to make the statement in the first place.

Following these guidelines, the writer might convert his short paragraph into a longer, more informative and persuasive one or develop two paragraphs, as I have below.

> Large classes can affect the learning of children. When class sizes exceed twenty, students do not receive the individual attention they need. They do not feel part of an identifiable group. They may become withdrawn. They may become distracted. If they do not understand a concept, they may not be able to let the teacher know. They fall farther and farther behind, and, in the end, they may reject the whole process of learning and suffer from a chronic lack of self-confidence.
>
> More will have to be invested to affect large classes. Additional money is the first necessity. Only extra funding can guarantee there are enough qualified teachers in our school system to reduce class sizes from their current high number. But more attention must also be paid to supporting staff and materials. It is no good merely providing enough teachers for sizes to drop to twenty or fewer. Libraries must have sufficient books to go around. Students must have easy access to computers on a regular basis.

No doubt you will have spotted at least some of my strategies for generating supporting ideas. All five of the sentences that I have added make the first paragraph support the assertion of the first sentence: that children's learning is affected if the size of the classes in which they are taught is too big. The supporting sentences either attempt to explain how and why that effect is produced or reiterate one of those explanations. In other words, I have identified what might be meant by large classes (over twenty) and then listed possible consequences of this problem: the lack of attention, withdrawal, distraction, and ultimate rejection.

The first two additional sentences of the second paragraph contribute in much the same way. The paragraph then turns on my use of the contrasting "But," just as did the examples from Galbraith and my former student. None of my suggestions lies beyond the reach or wit of the original writer. In fact, I'm sure that the writer must have had at least some of these ideas in mind when she wrote the original paragraph. How else could she have written it in the first place? Putting them on paper instead of leaving them in her imagination, so that the reader no longer has to infer her intentions, makes all of the difference. It changes simple assertions into a (potentially) convincing argument.

Now let's consider the second example more closely. This paragraph contains more sentences, and it's shaped more like our imagined tower than a pyramid already. Then below I have subsequently italicized words and phrases from the original that have cried out for development.

Example 2

> The number of students benefiting from higher education in the UK has risen dramatically during the last decade and now stands at nearly 50%. The reasons behind this rise in further education are both political and social, but the question on most people's lips today concerns who will pay tuition fees. Important and exciting changes are occurring, but the question of finance should not blind us to these opportunities. Everyone has the right to achieve their (sic) potential through education irrespective of cost. As Aristotle said, "Educated men are as much superior to uneducated men as the living are to the dead."

Example two presents us with a different but related problem, for here the paragraph appears to be developed well enough. Certainly length is not an issue. The paragraph clearly attempts to support its general claims more than the first example. But, despite that attempt, it consists mainly of unsupported assertions, each of which might serve as the basis for its own paragraph, either of the topic sentence or generated variety. Were we to unpick these claims and support them further with detailed ideas, we could turn our one paragraph into three or more and create the basis for an argumentative essay.

First, look at the expansion of sentence one. I've only added a possible explanation for the rise it mentions. Most of the explanation takes the form of facts, which, therefore, I have made up or left blank, though in an actual essay I would seek to confirm these facts.

The number of students benefiting from higher education in the UK has risen dramatically during the last decade and now stands at nearly 50%. In 1990, X number of students graduated from all of the universities in Great Britain. That figure represented only X% of all school leavers. In 2010, more than X% of school leavers or X enrolled, and X graduated. More than X% of those graduates were mature students for whom the dramatic expansion of higher education has meant a second chance to pursue their interests and to equip themselves with new skills.

We can then build a second paragraph by specifying the political and social reasons implied in the second sentence. In some cases, I have not just listed reasons, but I have also attempted to explain them. (For a wholly convincing explanation I would obviously need to do some research into the actual percentages involved.) Consider what relationship each sentence has to the one before it.

> *The reasons behind this rise in further education are both political and social.* Successive governments have realized that making higher education more accessible is necessary to meet the aspirations that middle and working class parents have for their children. Changing the status of what were polytechnics and providing all universities with incentives for widening participation wins votes. It is also good for the overall economy. The modern economy depends enormously on information and knowledge. Without a well-educated and motivated workforce equipped with basic skills of communication and problem solving, a country cannot compete in the global marketplace. It also cannot adapt well enough to the multiculturalism that globalization and mobility ensure. A well-educated population is always a more tolerant one.

The third sentence allows us to construct a paragraph using the contrasting model that we have seen before. The generation again involves further explanation, this time around the question about the responsibilities for paying fees.

> *But the question on most people's lips today concerns who will pay tuition fees.* To ask the taxpayer to foot the bill raises serious issues. Is it ethically right for someone who has not received the benefits of university education and the financial rewards that go with it to be required to pay for the privileges of those who do? Alternatively, passing along the cost to the individual student has problems, too. Won't the prospect of a large debt upon graduation deter precisely those people for whom expansion was designed? Can students really take advantage of the opportunity of higher education if they have to work long hours off campus just to pay for it?

My fourth paragraph could be split into two paragraphs, since the first sentence directs our attention to the "question of finance" after first citing the "important and exciting changes" that are "occurring." The sentence contains our contrasting signifier "but." I have only focused on the issue of finance and attempted to explain to the reader why she should not let that issue distract her from the "opportunities" potentially provided by the rise in student numbers. There is no right answer here, only better and worse development, greater or fewer degrees of persuasion. As long as you are guided by our mantras of specification, characterization, or explanation you can't really go wrong, assuming, of course, that your thinking is sound and honest. (And you have done your research where necessary.)

> *Important and exciting changes are occurring, but the question of finance should not blind us to these opportunities.* We should not lose sight of the fact that everyone benefits from widening participation. Society profits collectively from the increased earning powers of those who graduate from university and from the skills that they bring into the community. At the same time, however, we should remember that these same individuals earn more money over their lifetime than those without a degree. We should acknowledge also that graduates enjoy greater job satisfaction and are more adaptable to a rapidly changing environment.

My final paragraph develops and defends what seems to me the most important claim of the original paragraph: *Everyone has the right to achieve their (sic) potential through education irrespective of cost.* We might see this claim as the writer's expressed conclusion and later move it to the beginning as a thesis, as we would for an argumentative draft. For now, I have chosen to precede the claim with a statement of consequence derived from the paragraph above. I then follow the conclusion with restatements or reiterations, adding a supporting quotation to provide the weight of authority (Aristotle).

> We must therefore devise a compromise position that all parties can support and that recognizes both the benefits derived by those lucky enough to attend university and the rewards that those same people bring to the collective good. *Everyone has the right to achieve their (sic) potential through education irrespective of cost.* No one should be prevented from receiving higher education because they cannot afford to pay tuition fees. No one should be deterred due to a mountain of debt. As Aristotle said, "Educated men [and women] are as much superior to uneducated men [and women] as the living are to the dead."

Have a look now below. We have changed the initial paragraph into something resembling a mastermind draft, and, in the process, we have written a clearer, more concrete, and more convincing argument about the original topic. Read the new draft in its entirety and see what you think. When you have finished, copy and paste the conclusion in the last paragraph at the top of the draft and consider the structural effect and how you might revise the thesis you have created. Once you have finished Chapter 4 on formal introductory paragraphs you may even want to return to this draft and insert your thesis into the type of introduction that you think befits the topic best.

The Draft Essay

> *The number of students benefiting from higher education in the UK has risen dramatically during the last decade and now stands at nearly 50%.* In 1990, X number of students graduated from all of the universities in Great Britain. That figure represented only X% of all school leavers. In 2010, more than X% of school leavers or X enrolled and X graduated. More than X% of those graduates were mature students for whom the dramatic expansion of higher education has meant a second chance to pursue their interests and to equip themselves with new skills.
>
> *The reasons behind this rise in further education are both political and social.* Successive governments have

realized that making higher education more accessible is necessary to meet the aspirations middle class and working class parents have for their children. Changing the status of old polytechnics and providing all universities with incentives for widening participation wins votes. It is also good for the overall economy. The modern economy depends enormously on information and knowledge. Without a well-educated and motivated workforce equipped with basic skills of communication and problem solving a country cannot compete in the global marketplace. It also cannot adapt well enough to the multiculturalism that globalization and mobility ensure. A well-educated population is always a more tolerant one.

But the question on most people's lips today concerns who will pay tuition fees. To ask the taxpayer to foot the bill raises serious issues. Is it ethically right for someone who has not received the benefits of university education and the financial rewards that go with it be required to pay for the privileges of those who do? Alternatively, passing along the cost to the individual student has problems, too. Won't the prospect of a large debt upon graduation deter precisely those people for whom expansion was designed? Can students really take advantage of the opportunity of higher education if they have to work long hours off campus just to pay for it?

Important and exciting changes are occurring, but the question of finance should not blind us to these opportunities. We should not lose sight of the fact that everyone benefits from widening participation. Society profits collectively from the increased earning powers of those who graduate from university and from the skills that they bring into the community. At the same time, however, we should remember that these same individuals earn more money over their lifetime than those without a degree. We should acknowledge also that graduates enjoy greater job satisfaction and are more adaptable to a rapidly changing environment.

We must therefore devise a compromise position that all parties can support and that recognizes both the benefits derived by those lucky enough to attend university and the rewards that those same people bring to the collective good. *In conclusion, everyone has the right to achieve their (sic) potential through education irrespective of cost.* No one should be prevented from receiving higher education because they cannot afford to pay tuition fees. No one should be deterred due to a mountain of debt. As Aristotle said, "Educated men [and women] are as much superior to uneducated men [and women] as the living are to the dead."

EXERCISE 6: Generating Paragraphs

1. Read each sentence below and try to write a paragraph of a minimum of six sentences generated from that initial sentence.

2. With each example consider what abstract concept or general statement may need further explanation, elaboration, and/or illustration with specific details or examples.

3. The italicized word in the following example may give you a clue: My history teacher in secondary school was a *real inspiration* to me.

Examples

1. My parents consider using slang a sign of laziness and a symptom of a common apathy towards life.
2. My attitude towards politics has been influenced by several things.
3. I have traveled a long way from my roots to become the person I am today.

4. There are many reasons to vote for the political party that you prefer or a variety of reasons to abstain from voting altogether.

5. Choosing a career is not an easy decision.

6. "Fat" should not be a gender issue.

7. Saying that history repeats itself is far too simplistic.

8. After three hundred years, it is hardly surprising that an unreformed British monarchy is riddled with problems and anomalies.

9. Watching television encourages materialist values.

10. Despite all of the problems associated with it, the expansion of higher education is good for the country and its aspiring students.

EXERCISE 6a: Developing Paragraphs Fully

1. Choose a paragraph from the argumentative draft you have created through the previous exercises.

2. Try to improve that paragraph by developing it more completely, by explaining general claims or assertions more concretely.

3. Repeat step 2 for each of the paragraphs of your argumentative draft. Compare each to the original in the draft.

4. Now try a different tack. Take each sentence from one of the paragraphs in your original argumentative draft and see if you can build a complete essay by developing a separate paragraph from each of its sentences.

5. Repeat this second tack with the sentences of another paragraph. Do you think you are beginning to understand the concepts behind generating paragraphs well enough to apply that understanding consistently when revising your argumentative drafts?

Making Your Paragraphs More Coherent

"A good essay will march step by step to its destination. Each step will be clearly marked; it will depend on what has gone before, and it will lead gracefully to what comes after. Good transitions are essential to good writing."

(Richard Marius, *A Writer's Companion*, 3rd ed.)[15]

As our second sample paragraph above demonstrates, it's not enough simply to write longer paragraphs. We also need to give our paragraphs unity and structure, and, when you develop your paragraphs along the lines that we have just discussed, you will find that they normally achieve both aims. Your paragraphs will be unified, and they will have a structure. But giving your paragraphs unity and structure may not mean that they are sufficiently coherent. You may know how all of your ideas relate to one another and what holds them together overall, but your readers may not always be able to detect those relationships. For coherence often has as much to do with perception or visibility as with abstract concepts. That is, sentences cohere both syntactically through their sentence structures and semantically through explicit word choices, explicit forms of *connectives*.

There are a number of ways of achieving this explicit coherence. All require you to combine reading and editing skills with your writing skills. When you are freewriting or working on the mastermind draft of your essay, you will probably not want to think too long or too hard about your individual word choices. You will want to relax and get out of your own way to avoid hindering the flow of your ideas and your chances of genuine discovery. At these moments you are a writer, and a writer only, and you should write with as much confidence as you can, not worrying too much whether what you are saying is fully coherent or ideally phrased. However, once you relocate your conclusion and begin to revise your paragraphs, you must transform yourself. You must approach your essay as if you were its first and most astute, demanding reader.

You can't afford to be a lazy or an indifferent reader. You must be scrupulous, committed, and honest with yourself. You must identify not only places in the essay where your ideas may be unclear or do not hold together well enough but also those where they require still more explanation, and you must be prepared to take the time to correct those instances, sometimes re-ordering entire sections of your drafts if necessary. But you will always need to ensure that you include appropriate *transitional devices* so that your readers can follow your argument without hesitation or misunderstanding, without having to supply their own views, or getting lost along the way between thesis and conclusion.

Transitional Devices

As with my all of my advice about paragraphing, my suggestions about the use of transitional devices do not spring from some hypothetical notion of good writing or from any dogmatically held prejudice. They come from the observation of good writers. Good writers use a range of transitional devices – many, if not most, of them explicit – to help them retain the attention and understanding of their readers. Indeed, probably the most crucial difference between professional writers and less experienced ones lies in the meticulousness of the former ("In good writing, a reader finds it hard to get lost").[16]

In the past you may have had teachers who not only have *not* encouraged you to rely on such devices but who have also actively *discouraged* you, even imposing penalties if you did. The usual reason they give for such discouragement is that inserting connectives will either make your readers feel as if you are talking down to them, that you assume that they are too simple to follow your argument without such links, or reveal that you lack the ability to present a coherent argument without having to resort to such allegedly simple tools. Neither of these claims is valid, in my opinion, but, if you don't take my word for it, just have a look at the paragraphs of professional writers. Such writers are not, as a rule, simple. Neither do they patronize their readers. Yet the majority of them liberally use connectives of one type of another. Indeed, professional writers seem typically more aware of the need to keep their readers informed of the signs of their argument than non-professionals. Good writers know how imperative it is to make sure that their readers understand each point sufficiently and can understand their arguments without any trouble. "Readers," as Marius writes, need "a smooth bridge to carry them to their destination without unnecessary strain," and experienced writers know that it is impossible to persuade an audience if, at any time, a reader has to strain too much to follow their line of thought, if she doesn't understand at every stage what point they, as writers, are trying to make.[17]

For these reasons, I encourage you to use transitional devices explicitly, at least until you get the hang of them and your writing becomes almost instinctively connected, and so suitably coherent. In fact, I advise you to risk overusing them, if anything, at least initially in your drafts. Your motto for now should be "when in doubt, use a transitional device." Applying this motto will not only help you to write more coherent paragraphs, but it will also help you to discover more of your own ideas as you write. And you can always ditch these devices in your final draft if you are convinced that your sentences link together well enough in their absence, although I would not advise you to remove all of them. Indeed, a good way to check if sentences are sufficiently well connected is to see if you can insert a meaningful transitional device between them. If you can't without distorting the sense or making your ideas nonsensical, then clearly your ideas were not very well related to begin with. Another way is to read your essays aloud to yourself or to a friend. You will then instantly notice any gaps in thought or logic that should be bridged by a connective. Once you gain experience and confidence you may want to use connectives more implicitly. For now, however, it is best to play safe and always supply an explicit transitional device.

Common Transitional Devices

Transitional devices can take a variety of forms, but the most common ones convey some relationship of time or place or sequence. These are most often simple, one-word connectives or short phrases of the sort that you will notice sprinkled liberally as illustrations throughout these pages and the prose of other writers. The following represent some of the most useful of these transitional devices. No doubt you will remember most of them from earlier study.

Indeed	*Nevertheless*	*Moreover*	*Notwithstanding*
Nonetheless	*However*	*Therefore*	*For example*
As a result	*Thus*	*Alternatively*	*Instead*
By contrast	*Consequently*	*In fact*	*In short*
In conclusion	*Firstly*	*Similarly*	*In other words*
Secondly (etc.)		*On the other hand*	

The following sentences provide examples of good practice. As you read them, notice the way in which the writers punctuate their transitional devices. In Chapter 5, I will discuss punctuation in more detail, but an easy rule of thumb is to avoid all forms of punctuation except periods (full stops) or question marks unless you are absolutely certain you know the formal rules. If you are, then you will normally use commas after transitional devices that open sentences (except co-ordinating conjunctions) and place commas before and after ones that appear in the middle of sentences. You will always insert pairs of commas to set off phrases and clauses that appear in the middle of sentences. But, unless you know the rules and are absolutely certain that you know why you are using commas, don't use them anywhere, at least for now.

Examples of Sentences Using Common Transitional Devices

1. The theories of alchemy represent a curious confusion of genuine scientific insights with emotional, artistic, and religious considerations. *For example,* a typical alchemical theory was that gold might have been formed in the earth by the solidification of sunlight after it had been trapped by flowers and turned to nectar, then processed into honey by bees, then hardened by contact with the earth into sulphur. *Similarly,* it was thought silver might have been formed from moonlight, trapped into dewdrops and then changed by contact with the earth into quicksilver, finally being solidified to silver by pressure.

   (C.B. Cox, *The Twentieth Century Mind: History, Ideas and Literature in Britain*, Oxford: Oxford University Press, 1972, 312)

2. There is but one future we are all assured of, if you discount the certainty of taxes. But death is strangely

absent from contemporary discourses of the digital media, even those that focus on artificial life. Immortality of the soul rages as discursive formulation, but death has been banished. *However,* banishment is not destruction.

> (Sean Cubitt, "Supernatural futures: Theses on digital aesthetics,"*Future/Natural: Nature, Science, Culture,* ed. George Robertson, Melinda Mash, Lisa Tickner, Jon Bird, Barry Curtis and Tim Putman, Routledge: London and NY, 1996, 237)

3. Aristotle believed that no regime could satisfy man completely, and that the dissatisfaction would lead men to replace one regime with another in an endless cycle. Democracy did not occupy a special place in this sequence, either with respect to goodness or stability; *in fact,* both writers suggested that democracy had a tendency to give way to tyranny. *Moreover,* Aristotle did not assume the continuity of history. That is, he believed that the cycle of regimes was embedded in a larger natural cycle, whereby cataclysms like floods would periodically eliminate not only existing human societies, but all memory of them as well, forcing men to start the historical process over again from the beginning.

> (Francis Fukuyama, *The End of History and the Last Man,* Penguin Books: New York and London, 1992, 156)

4. The taste for quotations (and for the juxtaposition of incongruous quotations) is a Surrealist taste. *Thus,* Walter Benjamin – whose Surrealist sensibility is the most profound of anyone's on record – was a passionate collector of quotations.

> (Susan Sontag, *On Photography,* New York: Picador, 2001, 75)

5. It is curious that this not particularly attractive character [John Bull] should have endured so long. *After all,* he is neither physically appealing nor even particularly intelligent.

> (Jeremy Paxman, *The English: A Portrait of a People,* London: Michael Joseph, 1998, 185)

6. American society, as well as national social patterns in the American West, had reached [by the 1960s] new crossroads without being able to locate agreed-upon meeting points. *As a result,* westerners like California novelist Joan Didion, and many other Americans as well, concurred with postmodernists that Americans lacked a culture with a recognizable center.

> (Richard W. Etulain, *Reimagining the Modern American West: A Century of Fiction, History, and Art,* Tucson: University of Arizona Press, 1996, 141)

7. [Anthony] Crosland's idea of socialism was the spread of affluence and the decline of evident class distinctions. *Therefore* [Crosland] thought the United States the example of a society that was attaining a good attitude toward social equality.

> (Alan Sinfield, *Literature, Politics and Culture in Postwar Britain,* Oxford: Basil Blackwell Ltd., 1989, 253)

8. Often these different meanings were presented in terms of oppositions, such as natural versus artificial, nature versus reason, nature versus culture. These dichotomies are important for two reasons. *First,* they drew on old, often classical notions and were thus so deeply embedded in ways of thinking that they could not be used without self-consciousness as habitual, customary ideas which structured patterns of thought. *Second,* they had a marvelous capacity for containing contradictions. Raymond Williams, *for example,* has shown how this containment worked for the pair country versus city, where the former can be the valued element because people deemed it pure, natural and innocent. The country can equally be seen as negatively as wild, uncouth and barbaric yet also as 'natural.'

> (Ludmilla Jordanova, "Naturalizing the Family: Literature and the Bio-Medical Sciences in the Late Eighteenth Century," *Languages of Nature: Critical Essays on Science and Literature,* ed. L. Jordanova, London: Free Association Books, 1986, 86)

9. One of the most significant aspects of human development is that infants are born virtually helpless and experience a prolonged childhood. *Moreover*, as every parent knows, children go through an adolescent growth spurt, during which they put on inches at an alarming rate. Humans are unique in this respect: most mammalian species, including apes, progress almost directly from infancy to adulthood. A human adolescent about to embark on his or her growth spurt is likely to increase in size by about 25 percent. *By contrast*, the steady trajectory of growth in chimpanzees means that the adolescent adds only 14 percent to its stature by the time it reaches maturity.

(Richard Leaky, *The Origin of Humankind*, London: Weidenfeld & Nicolson, 1994, 44)

10. As democracy in America has expressed itself, the period 1900–25 is unparalleled in the importance of the role played by the average man. He was the principal spectator; *indeed*, he was the whole audience. He not only watched the performance, but largely determined the actions of those who from time to time were upon the stage, regulated the length of their tenure in the spotlight, retired them to the wings, or summoned them back. It was his will or his whim, his applause, his disapproval or his indifference that dictated the entrances and the exits. He himself was one of the performers – was *in fact* the principal performer in a more fundamental sense and more continuously than any of the actors; for the drama consisted essentially of the reactions of the average man to the actors and of the actors to him. This average man, this audience, was also in a true sense the author and the stage-manager. *In short*, he was, as he himself would express it, "pretty much the whole show."

(Mark Sullivan, *Our Times: The United States 1900–1925: The Turn of the Century*, New York and London: Charles Scribner's Sons, 1926, 1)

EXERCISE 6b: Using Transitional Devices Effectively

1. Pick one of your paragraphs from an earlier exercise or recent assessment.

2. Rewrite that paragraph using as many of the transitional devices above as you can appropriately.

3. Repeat the exercise.

4. Repeat the revision using transitional devices five more times before moving on. Make sure that you practice using a variety of devices and you use each one in a meaningful way.

Coordinating and Subordinating Conjunctions

Transitional devices also include coordinating and subordinating conjunctions. As their name suggests, coordinating conjunctions connect ideas of relatively equal weight or significance, although you don't need to remember the definitions of either of these types of connectives unless, of course, you want to impress your friends at a party. It's much more important that you use them effectively, and below is a list of coordinating conjunctions, all of which you will know.

And	*But*	*Or*	*For*	*Nor*	*Yet*	*So*

One issue involving coordinating conjunctions does deserve a special mention, however, if only because some conservative teachers of grammar, composition, and style often single out these types of connectives for special objection. Teachers of writing usually do not object to your using coordinating conjunctions in the middle of sentences or when they join two sentences together as in "We went to the seaside yesterday, and we ate ice cream while we were there" or "We went to the seaside yesterday to eat ice cream, but all of the ice cream shops were closed for the season." But sometimes these same teachers seem to have a major problem with coordinating conjunctions at the start of a sentence. Yet professionals often use "But" or "Yet" at the start of sentences rather than "however" in the middle, for example. Just look back at our earlier instances such as the one from Galbraith's paragraph. There are also times when it will be entirely appropriate to begin a sentence with "And" in order to stress a point. So don't be afraid to emphasize an idea by using a coordinating conjunction as a transitional device to begin a sentence. You will be in good company, as the examples below demonstrate. But accept this fact: you can always overdo a good thing. So develop your instincts and trust yourself.

Examples of Sentences Starting with a Coordinating Conjunction

1. American culture was always more in flux than its European counterparts. The opportunity to invent new categories of popular culture was open to American Jews with sufficient vision and capital as could never have been the case in Germany. Americans lacked the tradition of vicious anti-Semitism that erupted in murderous violence in medieval and modern Europe. *And* the speed of technological change favoured the enterprising and industrious newcomers.

   (David Lehman, *A Fine Romance: Jewish Songwriters, American Songs*, Nextbook: Schocken, New York, 2009, 168-9)

2. Eminent aestheticians have repeatedly declared that the highest form of song composition is a fusion of perfect poetry with perfect music. *But* actually a very powerful poem is apt to militate against all music.

   (Suzanne K. Langer, *Form and Feeling: A theory of art developed from Philosophy in a New Key*, New York: Charles Scribner's Sons, 1953, 153)

3. What is true of the novel is only a little less true of the essay. *For*, like the novel, the essay is a literary device for saying almost everything about almost anything. By tradition, almost by definition, the essay is a short piece, and it is therefore impossible to give all things full play within the limits of a single essay. *But* a collection of essays

91

can cover almost as much ground, and cover it almost as thoroughly as can a long novel.

> (Aldous Huxley, "The Essay," *Collected Essays*,
> New York: Harper & Row, 1959, 301)

4. *And* in so far as so many of De Quincey's stories seem to gravitate towards these most predictable and banal images of women, the sequence of what I have described so far might be seen, once again, in another light. *For* it is one of the attested responses to the problem of sexual difference that the woman, either fetishised as perfect or slandered as base, has to be endlessly punished for what the boy thinks he has discovered in her.

> (John Barrell, *The Infection of Thomas De Quincey:
> A Psychopathology of Imperialism*, New Haven
> and London: Yale University Press, 1991)

5. His was a garret room once again, and its little window had a pleasant prospect of a timber yard. *But* in comparison to what had gone before it seemed to him to be "a Paradise." *Yet* paradise had really been lost, and it was in this attic room that one night the young boy once more fell into a spasm which lasted until the morning.

> (Peter Ackroyd, *Dickens*, Reading: Vintage, 2002,
> 49-50)

EXERCISE 6c: Using Coordinating Conjunctions

1. Find five examples of paragraphs in which the writers include at least one coordinating conjunction as a transitional device.
2. Copy each paragraph in turn, reading each carefully for the content as well as for the style and placement of transitional devices.
3. Now write a paragraph of your own that incorporates one or more examples of a coordinating conjunction as an appropriate transitional device.
4. Reread the paragraphs you have revised for your argumentative draft. See if any of the transitions between pairs of sentences can be improved by adding a coordinating conjunction.

Subordinating Conjunctions

Subordinating conjunctions link ideas of differing order or merit, making one dependent or *subordinate* to the other. *Although, since, because, if, when, whenever, whoever,* and *whomever* are some subordinating conjunctions. Most often, however, subordinating conjunctions connect clauses and phrases within sentences rather than between them. They are vital for good writing, for it is virtually impossible to express complex ideas without resorting to complex sentences that require you to use subordinating conjunctions. But we won't discuss them in any detail now. They serve less as explicit transitional devices between sentences than as internal connectives, conveyors of relationships rather than signs of coherence.

EXERCISE 6d: Using Subordinating Conjunctions

1. Write five pairs of sentences joined by subordinating conjunctions.

2. Reread the paragraphs you have revised for your argumentative draft. Decide if any of the relationships between the ideas in any pair of sentences can be improved by the addition of a subordinating conjunction and connect those sentences explicitly with the appropriate one.

The Use of Repetition as a Transitional Device

We have discussed the value of reiteration overall, and various forms of repetition also serve as useful transitional devices. These forms are easy to use once you know what they are and how they function. They will enhance the coherence of your paragraphs and add more than a tad of sophistication to your writing.

Strict Repetition

The most obvious form of repetition is what we might call *strict repetition*, that is, repeating a word or phrase from one sentence at or near the beginning of the subsequent one, as in the following example: "Many feminists today worry that women have adopted methods of achieving power based on *the exploitation of sexuality* that they themselves had originally rejected. They find *this exploitation of sexuality* both demeaning and ineffective." Here is another example: "*Thin-slicing* is not an exotic gift. We *thin-slice* whenever we meet a new person or encounter a novel situation and have to make sense of something quickly. We *thin-slice* because we have to, and we come to rely on that ability because there are lots of situations where careful attention to the details of a very *thin slice*, even for no more than a second or two, can tell us an awful lot."

Earlier we saw a variation on this type of repetition in the student paragraph about *My Antonia*. That paragraph contained a form of strict repetition within a single sentence: "He longs to keep Antonia insulated from time and reality by creating the *perfect image* of her in his mind, even if maintaining *that image* means leaving her to her hardships with an empty promise to return." And here's a third and even easier example of an effective use of repetition you might become very familiar with indeed: "Below are five *sets of questions*. Each *set of questions* contains three *short answer questions*. You must answer two of these *short answer questions*."

Examples of Strict Repetition

1. I *simplify*, of course, but one is obliged to *simplify* Hegel since much of his work would otherwise remain impenetrably obscure.

   > (Frances Wheen, *Karl Marx*, London: Fourth Estate Limited, 1999, 22)

2. Recourse to the *pastoral* is an English mode of both fully gauging the calamities of the Great War and imaginatively protecting oneself against them. *Pastoral* reference, whether to literature or to actual rural localities and objects, is a way of invoking a code to hint by antithesis at

the indescribable; at the same time, it is a comfort in itself, like rum, a deep dugout, or a woolly vest. The Golden Age posited by Classical and Renaissance literary *pastoral* now finds its counterpart in ideas of "home" and "the summer of 1914." The language of literary *pastoral* and that of particular rural data can fuse to assist memory or imagination.

> (Paul Fussell, *The Great War and Modern Memory*, Oxford: Oxford University Press, 2000 (1975), 235)

3. What the framers of the First Amendment had in mind was *debate*, a great continuing *debate*, with the people hearing all sides and getting all the facts. If government could be kept from interfering with this *debate*, nothing could interfere with it; for a man who differed with the existing papers could start one of his own. The Founding Fathers did not foresee that 94 percent of American cities and eighteen American states would be without competing papers. In the overwhelming majority of communities there can now be no *debate* among rival editors. The editor in a one-paper town has the only voice there is, and the only one there is likely to be. The *debate* has become a soliloquy.

> (Robert Maynard Hutchins, "Argument and Persuasion," *Reading for Rhetoric: Applications to Writing*, 2nd ed., ed. by Caroline Shrodes, Clifford Josephson, James R. Wilson, New York: The Macmillan Company, 1967, 363)

4. The School System has much to say these days of the *virtue of reading* widely, and not enough about the *virtues of reading* less but in depth. There are any number of *reading* lists for *poetry*, but there is not enough talk about individual *poems*. *Poetry*, finally, is one *poem* at a time. To read any one *poem* carefully is the ideal preparation for *reading* another. Only a *poem* can illustrate how *poetry* works.

> (John Ciardi, "Robert Frost: The Way to the Poem," *Reading for Rhetoric: Applications to Writing*, 2nd ed., ed by Caroline Shrodes, Clifford Josephson, James R. Wilson, New York: The Macmillan Company, 1967, 333)

5. *History* began and prehistory ended when men learnt to read and write. Literate men produce a *civilization*, and almost every *civilization* has sought to extend its sway over others. Such is the essence of *Empire* and ancient *history* is a record of successive empires. *Empires* arose first in Egypt and Mesopotamia. The Old Testament tells the story of a people repeatedly conquered and yet surviving. The Medes, the Assyrians and the Persians all had their day.

> (A.P. Taylor, *Essays in English History*,
> London: Book Club Associates, 1977, 19)

Slant Repetition

You will, of course, want to vary your style of repetitions, and our second example we will refer to as *slant repetitions*, any form of slightly disguised repetition that is not exact but that nevertheless supplies a more-than-implicit link between sentences and ideas. Probably the clearest example involves *synonyms*, words that mean essentially the same thing though we spell them differently. "Loss" and "dispossession" in the first paragraph by Martin Corner represent examples of synonyms. So too do pairs of words such as "job" and "occupation," "view" and "opinion," "choice" and "selection," "delay" and "forestall." Substituting one synonym for a partner allows you to avoid the potential risk of monotony that might follow were you to rely too often or too heavily on strict repetition.

Examples of Slant Repetition

1. The decade from 1840 to 1850 had seen the *sharpest rise* in the city population of the United States, yet the *sharpest rise* of the century did not take place until after Mayo had written. During the decade from 1880 to 1890 there was a *dramatic leap* ahead, associated with large-scale immigration.

> (Asa Briggs, *Victorian Cities*, London: Penguin Books, 1963, 79-80)

2. From time to time, a *mutation* occurs that improves an *organism's* ability to cope with its environment. *Such a change* increases the likelihood that the *plantor animal* will be more successful and will win out in competing for such

essentials as food and mates against forms that are without the new advantage. (*Here are two sets of synonyms: "change" and "mutation" and "plant or animal" and "organism." The second not only varies the repetition but also in varying it potentially teaches the reader something: organisms include both plants and animals.*)

> (Sherwin B. Nuland, *The Wisdom of the Human Body*, London: Chatto and Windus, 1997, 136)

3. In recent years no new poet has so deeply impressed me with her imaginative flair or originality as Kay Ryan. I first saw *her poems* almost by accident. In 1994 a publisher gave me a *review copy* of *Flamingo Watching*, along with several other recent books. No critical fanfare accompanied the *slender volume*, and I had no special reason to think it possessed singular merit. But given the *work of an unfamiliar poet*, I always read a few poems, and I was immediately struck by the unusual compression and density of Ryan's work.

> (Dana Gioia, *Disappearing Ink: Poetry at the End of Print Culture*, Saint Paul, Minnesota: Greywolf Press, 2004, 135)

4. Many men are more *faithful* to their golf partners than to their wives, and have stuck with them longer. The *loyalty* we feel toward our chronic consorts in golf acquires naturally the mystical and eternal overtones that the wedding ceremony hopefully, and often vainly, invokes.

> (John Updike, *Golf Dreams: Writings on Golf*, London: Hamish Hamilton, 1996, 126)

5. *Giving time and money* to help others is a long and distinguished tradition in American society. Both *philanthropy* and *volunteering* are roughly twice as common among Americans as among the citizens of other countries. For the first several centuries of our national experience the social context for volunteering and philanthropy was primarily religious. *Caring for others* is a central tenet of our faiths. Toward the end of the nineteenth century a new theme became a more prominent part of the rationale for *altruism* – helping the less fortunate was a part of our civic duty.

> (Robert D. Putnam, *Bowling Alone: The Collapse and Revival of American Community*, New York: Touchstone Books, 2000, 117)

EXERCISE 6e: Using Repetition

1. Write five pairs of sentences linked by either strict or slant repetition. Try to include at least one example of each type of repetition among your five sentences.

2. Return to your argumentative draft and identify any instances where you could improve the coherence of your ideas by inserting transitions using strict or slant repetition.

Pronouns as Transitional Devices

Perhaps the most familiar form of slant repetition involves the common pronoun. Writers could hardly write without relying on words such as *it, he, she* (or *s/he*), *they, we, them* and *us*. The same can be said of slant repetitions such as common nouns for proper nouns: "woman" for "Hillary Clinton" or "man" for "George Clooney." These simple forms of slant repetition are second nature to us. I mention them here only to remind you of the importance of keeping their references clear, of making sure that the antecedent of your pronouns – the noun to which your pronoun refers – is always obvious and unambiguous.

Be particularly careful with your pronoun references when you use them with possessives. We have all seen people write a sentence like this one: "The president's cabinet never seems to contradict him." We think we know what that sentence means and to what "him" refers. But, in actual fact, a pronoun can only refer to a noun, and, in this case, "president's" is a possessive adjective, not a noun (the cabinet of the president). To be correct, the sentence ought to read either "The cabinet of the president never seems to contradict him" or "His cabinet never seems to contradict the president." Similarly, you should change a sentence such as "In Madonna's career, she has shown an uncanny ability not only to anticipate trends but to exploit them" to "In her career, Madonna has shown an uncanny ability not only to anticipate trends but to exploit them." For the same reason, this sentence – "None of Sartre's opponents adequately answered his arguments"– is clearer when written in this way: "None of the opponents of Sartre adequately answered his arguments."

EXERCISE 6f: Using Pronouns as Transitions

1. Write five pairs of sentences that include a pronoun as a transitional device.

2. Reread the paragraphs you have revised for your argumentative draft. Decide whether any of the transitions between pairs of sentences can be improved by substituting a pronoun for a proper noun or whether you can improve any sentences by rephrasing them so that you can insert a pronoun as a transitional device.

Parallelism as a Means of Transition

There are also less obvious and more sophisticated forms of repetition you can learn to use. Indeed, classical rhetoric contains an array of formal devices and tropes, most of which are unpronounceable, for various types and degrees of repetitions. One reasonably simple form of slant repetition is signified by the rhetorical term *parallelism.*

Parallelism refers to the use of the same basic sentence construction in consecutive sentences: "*Mary ran* to meet Joe. *She threw* her arms around him. *She told* him how much she loved him. *She invited* him in for tea." All four sentences conform to the same initial pattern: an opening noun ("Mary") or pronoun ("She") followed by a simple verb ("ran," "threw," "told," "invited") and an explanatory phrase. This structural conformity is a form of slant repetition, and it acts as a transitional device by binding together the sentences and the ideas they express.

We saw its effect in the earlier paragraph about Willa Cather: "*Jim may refuse* to marry a socially and sexually disgraced woman, or *he may desire* to pursue a successful career. Or *he may simply fear* sex and sexuality." And I might add this example, involving the imperative construction (imperative sentences give orders, by the way): "If you are not prepared to revise, you might as well *save yourself some time* right now and *close this book. Go watch television. Text a friend. Take a walk. But don't kid yourself.*"

Examples of Parallelism: Parallel Sentence Construction

1. Some people dislike the word *argument* because it sounds too pugnacious. But it is a civilized term; *we make arguments* instead of war. *We persuade people* rather than beat them into submission. Democracy depends on argument. *Candidates argue* that they are more qualified than their opponents; *representatives argue* that their policies are better than the alternatives. *Lawyers and judges argue* about what the laws mean. *Citizens argue* with each other about what's right or wrong with society. In tyrannies, *people don't argue* – at least not in public. Democracy is unending disputation.

   > (Richard Marius, *A Writer's Companion*, 3rd ed., New Baskerville: R.R. Donnelley & Sons Company, 1995, 61)

2. I realized another thing, that in this world *fast runners do not always win* the race, and *the brave do not always win* the battle. *Wise men do not always earn* a living, *intelligent men do not always get* rich, and *capable men do not always rise* to high positions. Bad luck happens to everyone. You never know when your time is coming. Like birds suddenly caught in a trap, like fish caught in a net, we are trapped in some evil moment when we least expect it.

   > (Ecclesiastics 9, 11: *Good News Bible*, Swindon: Collins, 1976, 656)

3. *There is no life* in the fossil. *There is no life* in the carbon in my body. As the idea strikes me – and believe me it comes as a profound shock – I run down the list of elements. *There is no life* in the iron, *there is no life* in the phosphorus, the nitrogen does not contain me; the water that soaks my tissues is not I. What am I then? I pinch my body in a kind of sudden desperation. My heart knocks, my fingers close around the pen. *There is, it seems, a semblance* of life here.

   > (Loren Eiseley "The Uncomplicated Man," *Reading for Rhetoric Applications to Writing*, 2nd ed., Caroline Shrodes, Clifford Josephson, James R. Wilson, eds., New York: The Macmillan Company, 1967, 236-7)

4. *We shall* go on to the end; *we shall fight* in France; *we shall fight* on the seas and oceans; *we shall fight* with growing confidence and growing strength in the air; *we shall defend* our island, whatever the cost may be; *we shall fight* on the beaches, *we shall* fight on the landing grounds, *we shall* fight in the fields and in the streets; *we shall* fight in the hills; *we shall* never surrender, and even if, which I do not for a moment believe, this island or a large part of it were subjugated and starving, then our empire beyond the seas, armed and guarded by the British fleet, would carry on the struggle, until, in God's good time, a new world, with all its powers and might, steps forth to the rescue and the liberation of the old.

> (Winston Churchill, "Wars are not won by Evacuations," *Winston Churchill His Complete Speeches 1899-1963, Vol. VI 1935-1942*, ed. Robert Rhodes James, New York, N.Y.: Chelsea House Publications, 1974, 6231)

5. *Africans want to be paid* a living wage. *Africans want to perform* work which they are capable of doing, and not work which the government declares them to be capable of. *Africans want to be allowed* to live where they obtain work, and not be endorsed out of an area because they were not born there. *Africans want to be allowed* to own land in places where they work, and not to be obliged to live in rented houses which they can never call their own. *Africans want to be part* of the general population, and not confined to living in their own ghettoes.

> (Nelson Mandela, "An Ideal for which I am Prepared to Die," *Nelson Mandela The struggle is my life*, London: IDAF Publications Ltd., 1990, 180)

EXERCISE 6g: Using Parallelism

1. Write five paragraphs that contain parallel constructions.
2. Reread the paragraphs you have revised for your argumentative draft. See if you can enhance their sense of coherence or development by creating parallel constructions.

Polyptotons: Having Fun with Rhetoric and Transitions

Any book with *rhetorical* in its subtitle is probably obliged to include one unpronounceable device for creating coherence, at least, and my overwhelming favorite for inclusion (because it works so well!) is the *polyptoton*, pronounced **Po – Lip – Toe – Ton.** (Type the word out on your computer, and I guarantee it will be marked by that jagged red line that is meant to tell you that the word in question is misspelled, although in this case your computer is wrong.) "Polyptoton" refers to two words that derive from the same root but appear in different forms and with different endings such as "conform" and "conformity," which I used a few pages ago. I don't introduce the polyptoton just for the sake of it. I include it because it is deceptively simple to use, for one thing, and, for another, learning about it will help you remember the principle and importance of transitional devices. It will also give you a chance to include a sophisticated form of repetition, as no less a writer than Shakespeare shows when he writes in Sonnet 121 that "All men are *bad,* and in their *badness* reign" or when he writes the following lines in Sonnet 116:

> Let me not to the marriage of true minds
> Admit impediments. Love is not love
> Which *alters* when it *alteration* finds,
> Or bends with the *remover* to *remove*

Other examples might be "magic" and "magician" or "supervise" and "supervision." "Democracy" and "democratic" is another example. So too are "essay" and "essayist," "teacher" and "taught," and "student" and "studying" or "studious." In our first paragraph example, Martin Corner used polyptotons when he connected his sentences and ideas by moving between "loss" and "lose" and "lost" and between "dispossess" and "dispossession." And, in my explanation of slant repetition, I created a polyptoton by following "substitute" with "substitution." Later, when defining "polyptoton" itself, I used "include" and "inclusion." (Don't say you didn't notice.) Some of the earlier examples of strict repetition include polyptotons, and many of my students have grown to enjoy polyptotons as much as I do. It's fun just to say the word, and once you've learned to spell it you will never forget either the figure or how to use it.

Examples of Polyptotons as Transitional Devices

1. Experience has demonstrated all too fully that any ack-nowledgement of gender-based difference was almost inevitably employed as a justification for *exclusion*. Either it was used to *exclude* them (women) from science or to brand them as "not women" in practice, and usually both at the same time.

> (Evelyn Fox Keller, "The Gender/Science System: or Is Sex to Gender as Nature is to Science?," *Feminism and Science*, ed. Nancy Turner, Bloomington and Indianapolis: Indiana University Press, 1989, 35)

2. *Revolutions* do not always turn out well. To *revolt* at any time, to any degree, requires a lot of nerve, and the help of fellow *revolutionaries*. (author)

3. The *destructive* instability of the feminine can be settled, stablised, only by being *destroyed*, but even in death it continues to *destroy*.

> (John Barrell, *The Infection of Thomas De Quincey: A Psychopathology of Imperialism*, New Haven London: Yale University Press, 1991, 102)

4. The method of textual *interpretation* gives the *interpreter* a certain leeway. He can choose and emphasize as he pleases. It must naturally be possible to find what he claims in the text. My *interpretations* are no doubt guided by specific purpose.

> (Erich Auerback, *Mimesis: The Representation of Reality in Western Literature*, translated by Willard R. Trask, Princeton: Princeton University Press, 1991 (1953), 556)

5. The youthful *owner* becomes, unconsciously, a philosopher. It is the sense of *ownership* which appeals most strongly to his untutored and undisciplined nature. The quest of the beautiful, the desire to excel in the art of gardening, the determination to induce the soil to yield its richest treasures at his behest are a later development of his maturer years. But the consciousness of *ownership* and the desire for pleasure are among the earliest characteristics of childhood, and so

sure a foothold do they obtain that the onward march of after years neither obliterates nor eradicates them.

> (F. Hadfield Farthing, F.R.H.S., *Saturday in my Garden*, London: Grant Richards, Ltd., 1911, 15)

6. We've seen that *imprisonment* rates are not determined by crime rates so much as the differences in official attitudes towards punishment versus rehabilitation and reform. In societies with greater inequality, where the social distances between people are greater, where attitudes of "us" and "them" are more entrenched and where lack of trust and fear of crime are rife, public and policy makers alike are more willing to *imprison* people and adopt punitive attitudes towards the "criminal elements" of society. More unequal societies are harsher, tougher places. And as *prison* is not particularly effective for either deterrence or rehabilitation, then a society must only be willing to maintain a high rate (and high cost) of *imprisonment* for reasons unrelated to effectiveness.

> (Richard Wilkinson and Kate Pickett, *The Spirit Level: Why More Equal Societies Almost Always Do Better*, London: Allen Lane, 2009, 55)

7. I hate to *insist* so strongly that you practice your writing, but I am afraid that *insistence* is necessary. (author)

8. A *sustainable* world would need rules, laws, standards, boundaries, social agreements, and social constraints, of course, as does every human culture. Some of the rules for *sustainability* would be different from the rules people are used to now. Some of the necessary controls are already coming into being as, for example, in the international ozone agreement and the greenhouse gas negotiations. But rules for *sustainability*, like every workable social rule, would be put in place not to destroy freedoms, but to create freedoms or to protect them.

> (Donella Meadows, Jorgen Randers, Dennis Meadows, *Limits to Growth*, London and Stirling, VA: Earthscan, 2006, 257)

9. The *creative* writer does the same as the child at play. He *creates* a world of phantasy which he takes very seriously – that is, which he takes with large amounts of emotion – while separating it sharply from reality.

(Sigmund Freud, "Writers and Day-Dreaming,"
Art and Literature, London: Penguin Books, 1986,
132)

10. Practice may not "make *perfect*," but it will take you closer to *perfection* than anything else I know. (author)

EXERCISE 6h: Using Polyptotons

1. Choose ten words and create as many sets of polyptotons as you can.

2. Use each set to link two meaningful sentences together.

3. Find ten examples of polyptotons in the writing of others.

4. Write two sentences linked together by each of these sets of polyptotons.

5. Now add a third sentence with a third polyptoton to each of your examples in number 4.

6. Identify instances in your argumentative draft where you might use appropriate polyptotons to improve the transitions between sentences.

Reiteration: Restatement as Transitional Device

Polyptotons represent only one end of the spectrum of forms of repetition that characterize good writing. What are examples, for example, but reiteration? What do supporting quotations represent, if not reiteration? And reiterating (like using polyptotons) comes easily, once you are alert to its advantages and its naturalness. Don't we all repeat ourselves all of the time? Don't we often ask others to do the same thing, to explain themselves, to tell us "in other words?" What else, too, are we doing but repeating ourselves when we use an analogy to make our points, when we phrase our words differently but say essentially the same thing, as in the last two sentences in the paragraph below?

> Railtrack, the postal service, air traffic control and the London Underground are not one-off problems, requiring ad hoc solutions. They are aspects of the general problem of finding structures for the efficient provision of public services. Nationalization of utilities, although not a successful policy, was not adopted through sheer perversity. *The issues which led to it have not gone away. The opportunities to find better long term solutions are still there to be taken.*[18]

So don't hesitate to repeat yourself at times, no matter what you have been told in the past. The advice that Fairbairn and Winch offer about stating the obvious in *Reading, Writing and Reasoning: A Guide for Students* is equally true about using forms of repetition and reiteration: "Do not be afraid of patronizing your readers by supplying information, references or arguments you think are obvious because they may not be obvious (to others)."[19] The writers below from whom I have taken models of good practice are surely not patronizing their readers.

Examples of Reiteration for Transitions

1. Psychoanalysis is the art of making interest out of interest that is stuck. We don't, in other words, believe that the football fan isn't really interested in football. We believe that he is far more interested in football than he can let himself know. In psychoanalysis we treat the objects of interest as clues and cues, as commas that look like full stops. Every object of desire is an obscure object of desire, leading us to ask both why this rather than that, and why anything at all? Free-floating attention itself, as a method, is a tribute to the vagaries of interest. Evenly hovering attention wants to land. There is, *that is to say*, as Freud implies, a will to interest that can usurp a capacity for it.

   (Adam Phillips, *The Beast in the Nursery*, London: Faber & Faber, 1998, 14)

2. It's necessary to understand at the outset that BAD language is not bad, like "shit" or "motherfucker." It's more like "gaming" for "gambling," "taupe" for "mouse gray," "starters" for "appetizers," "shower activity" for "rain," "nonperforming loans" for "bad debts," and "preexisting" (or "resale") home for "used home." *That is,*

there must be in the language, as there is not in, say, "fuck," an impulse to deceive, to shade the unpleasant or promote the ordinary to the desirable or the wonderful, to elevate the worthless by a hearty laying-on of the pretentious.

> (Paul Fussell, *BAD, or, The Dumbing of America*, New York: Simon & Schuster, 1991, 10)

3. By letting the reader discover and distinguish the variety of visual facts that make up the impressions of labyrinthine light and shadow, [John] Ruskin both alerts him to the presence of similar facts in other scenes – conveys a particular painterly way of seeing – and demonstrates the kind of orderly optical scanning by which a spectator fully sees a picture or scene. What the writer describes, *in other words*, is the scene as it is discovered by the spectator.

> (Elizabeth K. Helsinger, *Ruskin and the Art of the Beholder*, Cambridge: Harvard University Press, 1982, 20)

4. Aristotle did not assume the continuity of history. *That is*, he believed that the cycle of regimes was embedded in a larger natural cycle, whereby cataclysms like floods would periodically eliminate not only existing human societies, but all memory of them as well, forcing men to start the historical process over again from the beginning. In the Greek view, history thus is not secular but cyclical. (Notice the polyptotons: "history" / "historical cycle" / "cyclical.")

> (Francis Fukuyama, *The End of History and the Last Man*, New York and London: Penguin Books, 1992, 56)

5. As a wishing animal that wants only gratification, if possible instantly, the human animal needs to defend itself against its most longed-for pleasures, both sexual and aggressive, pleasures unacceptable without at least some controls. It is first the society of the child – its parents, siblings, teachers, priests – and internalized prohibitions acquired from a wider world that sets limits on passions. The less one knows about one's demanding appetites, the better. *In short*, this [point] is particularly relevant to the historian – the individual's imperious desires and the needs of civilization are usually at odds. All education, whatever else it might be, is also a stringent imposition of

unwelcome boundaries.

(Peter Gay, *The Naked Heart: The Bourgeois Experience: Victoria to Freud, Volume IV*, London: Harper Collins, 1995, 9)

EXERCISE 6i: Using Reiteration

Write two paragraphs, each of which includes one or more examples of reiteration used as a transitional device.

Another Look at Transitional Devices

Let's look now at an example of a well-developed, coherent paragraph that incorporates various forms of connectives. The paragraph comes from an essay by Andrew Bennett and Nicholas Royle entitled "Racial Difference."[20] I have revised the essay slightly for those of you who have never read the novel *Jane Eyre* in order to dramatize the elements we have been talking about, and I have highlighted various transitional devices in a second version that follows. But, first, see if you can identify the various types before you look down at the annotated version.

Example 1

Charlotte Bronte's *Jane Eyre* (1847) is one of the classic nineteenth-century novels in English. It describes a love affair between the eponymous heroine, a governess, and her aristocratic master, Rochester. The novel ends with the marriage of Jane and Rochester after Jane has become both professionally and economically independent. Jane's struggle for independence marks the novel as centrally engaged with the oppression of women in nineteenth-century England and with the possibility of their liberation from constricting roles of subservience to their male 'masters.' Alongside the question of gender, however, *Jane Eyre* raises other questions. These are questions of racial difference and they form the focal point of this chapter. Jane and Rochester are unable to marry because Rochester is already married to Bertha Mason, a Creole woman from the West Indies. This woman, who is mad, is kept locked up in Rochester's attic. Occasionally she escapes, and at one point attempts to set light to Rochester's bed while he is in it. Finally, in a pyromaniacal frenzy, she sets light to the house and dies in the blaze. Her death leaves the way clear for Jane and Rochester to marry, although not before Rochester is blinded and crippled in trying to save Bertha from the fire.

Now read the version that follows. I have placed key transitional devices in bold print and briefly identified them for you.

Example 1 revised

Charlotte Bronte's *Jane Eyre* (1847) is one of the classic nineteenth-century novels in English. **It (*pronoun*)** describes a love affair between the eponymous heroine, a governess, and her aristocratic master, Rochester. **The novel (*noun referring to pronoun and original proper noun Jane Eyre*)** ends with the marriage of Jane and Rochester after Jane has become both professionally and economically **independent**. Jane's struggle for **independence (*I wonder whether Bennett and Royle realized they were using a polyptoton*)** marks the novel as centrally engaged with the oppression of women in nineteenth-century England and with the possibility of their liberation from constricting roles of subservience to their male 'masters.' Alongside **the question of gender, (*summation/reiteration as with our use of "this" and a clarifying phrase*) however (*relational transition device*)**, *Jane Eyre* raises **other questions (*strict repetition*)**. These are **questions of racial difference (*strict repetition combined with summation/ reiteration*)** and **they (*pronoun*)** form the focal point of this chapter. Jane and Rochester are unable to marry because Rochester is already married to **Bertha Mason**, a Creole woman from the West Indies. **This woman (*repetition substitution common noun for proper noun*)**, who is mad, is kept locked up in Rochester's attic.

Occasionally **she** (*pronoun*) escapes, and at one point attempts to **set light** to Rochester's bed while **he** (*pronoun – though notice here that the antecedent is Rochester's and therefore an adjective rather than a noun*) is in it. **Finally** (*transitional device*), in a pyromaniacal frenzy, she **sets light** (*strict repetition*) to the house and **dies** in the blaze. **Her death** (*polyptoton: "dies" and "death"*) leaves the way clear for Jane and Rochester to marry, **although** (*subordinate conjunction*) not before Rochester is blinded and crippled in trying to save Bertha from the **fire** (*synonym*).

Here is another example, again slightly revised, taken from a paragraph in an essay entitled "Myth and Ritual in Shakespeare."[21] I think we all know who Shakespeare is and I'm sure you've heard of *Othello*, even if you've never read it. Try to identify as many transitional devices as you can before I explain each sentence below.

Example 2

Everywhere in Shakespeare there is a passion which is primarily the copy of a model, a passion that is destructive not only because of its sterile rivalries but because it dissolves reality. This ubiquitous passion tends to the abstract, the merely representational. Its model may be present in the flesh and strut on the stage of the theatre. It may also rise from the pages of the book, come out of the frame of a picture, turn into the worship of a phantom, verbal or iconic. But it is always a text. It is Othello's heroic language, the real object of fascination for Desdemona rather than Othello himself. It is the portrait of Portia which her lover chooses to contemplate in preference to the original. Whatever its specific form, Shakespeare's metaphysical passion is a corruption of life, always open to the corruptive suggestion of mediators and go-betweens such as Pandarus of *Troilus and Cressida*.

Now see if you understand the role of each sentence and connective in the same way I have emphasized below.

Example 2: Explanation of the Relationships Between and Among Ideas and Sentences

1. Everywhere in Shakespeare there is a passion which is primarily a copy of a model,

    (The initial general claim)

2. a passion that is destructive not only because of its sterile rivalries but because it dissolves reality.

    (The initial claim is here clarified further, partly through the introduction of a reason, signaled by the subordinate conjunction "because.")

3. This ubiquitous passion tends to the abstract, the merely representational.

    (The transition and link are supplied by the use of "this" as a demonstrative adjective and a clarifying phrase: "This ubiquitous passion." "Ubiquitous" refers back to the opening claim about the passion that is a copy of a model being present "everywhere" in Shakespeare, "ubiquitous" meaning, of course, to exist in all places. There is also an exact repetition of the word "passion.")

4. Its model may be present in the flesh and strut on the stage of theatre.

    (The repetition of the word "model" from the opening sentence allows this sentence to work with the preceding one to illustrate or confirm the claim of the initial sentence.)

5. It may also rise from the pages of the book, come out of the frame of a picture, turn into the worship of a phantom, verbal or iconic.

    (The use of "also" signals that this sentence provides another example of the places in which models exist. In fact, it gives us three or four. "May also rise" establishes a sentence construction that duplicates the one for the preceding sentence: "may be present.")

6. But it is always a text.

("But" allows for a transition as contrast, much as we saw earlier in our sample paragraphs.)

7. It is Othello's heroic language, the real object of fascination for Desdemona rather than Othello himself.

(A specific example backs up this contrasting, second claim. The example serves as an explanation by way of illustration.)

8. It is the portrait of Portia which her lover chooses to contemplate in preference to the original.

(A second example explains by illustrating. Notice how this second example provides additional coherence because it repeats the syntax – the sentence structure – of the sentence before it. The two sentences are also similar in construction: "It is.")

9. Whatever its specific form, Shakespeare's metaphysical passion is a corruption of life, always open to the corruptive suggestion of mediators and go-betweens such as Pandarus of Troilus and Cressida.

(The first phrase of this sentence – "Whatever its specific form"– connects it to the three before it and sums up the writer's position initiated by the contrasting statement in the middle of the paragraph. "Shakespeare's metaphysical passion" reiterates the idea that the passion which is a copy of a model is "everywhere" in Shakespeare, that it is "ubiquitous." And, finally, within the sentence we find an example of a polyptoton: "corruption" and "corruptive.")

Using "This" with a Clarifying Phrase

These examples of reiteration demonstrate that good writing occasionally requires us to sum up, to remind our readers what we have said and what conclusions we may have reached so far. And, with that advice in mind, there is one more form of connective that I especially encourage you to adopt. It involves the use of the word *this*. "This" can serve either as a demonstrative adjective, as in *"This* cute little kitten" and *"This* pedantic little man"*, or as a demonstrative pronoun, as in *"This* makes me really angry." The first use causes no problems. Writers need demonstrative adjectives to help them distinguish among objects and ideas. My concern is for the latter case. In such instances, "this" generally refers to some preceding idea. Yet it remains simply a meager, abstract demonstrative. The idea to which it is meant to refer has only been implied in the earlier sentences. As a consequence, the reader cannot possibly know precisely to what "this" refers (what its antecedent is).

This lack of certainty means that the reader is left to infer the intended antecedent herself from the earlier sentences. (Remember: readers "infer." Writers and speakers "imply" their ideas: President Bush strongly *implied* a connection between Iraq and international terrorism. The public *inferred* from his comments that an invasion of Iraq was justified. Or the *inference* from his comments was that the invasion of Iraq was justified.) The result is confusion, at best, and, at worst, a complete breakdown of communication. For, if your antecedent is missing, your reader will supply one, if only unconsciously, and, nine times out of ten, the one she supplies will not be the one you may have planned. Often writers don't have one in mind when they use the pronoun. Indeed, usually a writer uses "this" as a demonstrative pronoun because he has not taken the time to ask himself exactly what it is he does have in mind. Consider this example.

> The Federal Communications Commission, the F.C.C., has been steadily lifting restrictions on cross-ownership of media and communications companies. The day when a single conglomerate could own your local newspaper, several of your local TV channels, your cable company and your phone company – and offer your only route to the Internet – may not be far off. The result of *this* will probably be exorbitant access charges, but that's the least of it. What happens when a few media conglomerates control not only what you watch, but what you can download?[22]

The writer is an internationally noted economist and an excellent writer, and, when we first read through his paragraph, we may initially think we know to what exactly his "this" refers. It surely has something to do with the situation that he describes in the preceding two sentences. And we assume he does not particularly like that situation. So it may well be that he expects us to infer such criticism and to supply the words "bad situation" immediately after "this," so that the sentence reads implicitly as "The result of this bad situation will be exorbitant access charges..."

You might think such an inference would follow so naturally that there is little harm in the writer's not supplying the phrase himself. But suppose you are a member of the board of trustees for one of these conglomerates. Your reading might be different. You might supply something like "necessary development" or "benign result of global capitalism" as in "The result of this necessary development will be exorbitant access charges, but that's the least of it." Given the difference in sense that results from these possible inferences, shouldn't the writer anticipate some skeptics in his audience? More crucially, should he not seize the opportunity here to be more, rather than less, precise, to sum up his preceding ideas while giving his readers an unfailing sign about the direction of his argument? What about "this inappropriate consolidation of assets" or "this example of deregulation gone mad?" I feel uncomfortable trying to put words into the head of such an experienced writer. But he's left me little choice as a reader.

You can avoid such problems of misdirection and ambiguity very simply, however, if you stick to this one easy rule: *never use "this" by itself as a demonstrative pronoun. Use it only with a clarifying word or phrase*, such as "This mistaken use of the adjective "this" always confuses me." If you do, you will not write a pair of sentences like this one: "Jack has not made up his mind whether to attend university or spend a gap year traveling around the world. This has worried him endlessly." You will instead write one like either of these pairs: "Jack has not made up his mind whether to attend university or spend a gap year traveling around the world. This inability to reach a decision has worried him endlessly" or "Jack has not made up his mind whether to attend university or spend a gap year traveling around the world. This choice between two such different opportunities has worried him endlessly." Or you might even write "This simple choice between expected behavior and un-bridled freedom has worried him endlessly."

But don't take my word only. Keep an eye out for instances of both good and bad practice with "this"and see for yourself the difference a clarifying phrase can make. What, for example, do you think we are meant to think "this" signifies in the following passage?[23]

> The past 30 years have been a golden age for the mass invention of emotionally skewed historical untruths and myths. Some of them are a public danger. I am thinking of countries like India under the BJP, the US, Silvio Berlusconi's Italy, not to mention many of the new nationalisms, with or without fundamentalist religious reinforcement. *This* produces endless claptrap on the fringes of nationalist, feminist, gay, black and other in-group histories, but it has also stimulated interesting new historical developments in cultural studies, such as what has been called the "memory boom in history." (Note the polyptotons: "national-isms" / "nationalist", "histories" / "historical" / "hist-ory.")

By contrast, the passage below, in which "this" and "these" serve as demonstrative adjectives that precede clarifying phrases, is surely much clearer because it leaves so much less for the reader to infer.

> The historical interests of most Marxist historians were not so much in the Base – the economic infrastructure – as in the relations of base and superstructure. *This socio-economic current* was wider than Marxism. *These historical modernizers* asked the same questions and found themselves engaged in the same intellectual battles, whether inspired by human geography, Weberian sociology or the Marxism of the communist historians who became carriers of historical modern-ization in Britain. (Note the polyptotons: "moderniz-ers"/"modernizations", "historical" / "historians.")

And he's likely to be more persuasive as he continues here, and for the same reasons.

> They all saw each other as allies against historio-graphical conservatism, even when they represented mutually hostile positions. *This front of progress* advanced from the Second World War to the 1970s.

The following examples illustrate just how much clearer your ideas can become – and how much more coherent your transitions will be – when you follow your use of the word "this" with an explicit clarifying phrase.

Examples of Good Transitions: "This" with a Clarifying Phrase

1. A few days after my daughter's birth I go to a concert. I had bought the tickets weeks before, not expecting her to come so soon. I have difficulty walking because of my scar, and my grasp of the principles of breastfeeding is still tentative, but nevertheless I am determined to go. During pregnancy I had plenty of time to formulate stirring resolutions concerning the maintenance in motherhood of my independence and interests, fervently imagining myself at parties and gala events, skiing in the Bundeswald, reclining in Mediterranean sunsets, sitting meditatively at my desk, all the while with the baby in a sort of cartoon thought-bubble above my head. *This state of mind* has extended briefly into my daughter's life like a projection of rock overhanging the cliff. My mother-in-law is to hand to assist with the transition and appears nervous.

   (Rachel Cusk, *A life's work: on becoming a mother*, London: Fourth Estate, 2001, 85)

2. Another aspect of the "happy hours" that children spent with Lewis Carroll, apart from the nonsense tales, was his flair for unobtrusive instruction given on walks and while being photographed. *This kind of palatable learning*, common in every nursery school today, was unheard of in the 1860s.

   (Mavis Batey, *Stories behind Stories: The Adventures of Alice*, New York: Macmillan, 1998, 28-9)

3. At my school a lot of what I learned about religion felt more like an imposition of ideas about how a person should be rather than a guide to a greater understanding of myself and my own spirituality. I found my thoughts and actions were therefore significantly affected by what my religious teaching considered the right way to think and the right way to behave. *This pressure* encouraged me to perceive of God as a vindictive, authoritative, controlling, and manipulative figure who deprived me of my freedom, inner peace and authenticity. To live a God-fearing life under the relentless scrutiny of such an omnipresent force ever ready to judge and punish me felt like a psychological prison, a kind of death in life much in the way that Philip Larkin portrays the experience of the speaker in his poem "High Windows." The poem expresses the speaker's desire to liberate himself from an oppressive figure of God, the enforcer of an outside system of belief. His rise above this systematic oppression, the poem implies, happens once the speaker finds the will to think for himself.

> (Adapted from an essay by a Kingston University undergraduate)

4. Benjamin Franklin, a leading example of an enlightened North American Mercantilist writer, was highly optimistic about the ultimate place of America within the British Empire. He saw the old world nearly fully populated and the new as brimming with undeveloped resources and opportunities. It was necessary in America mainly to think how best to exploit the open spaces. Franklin was confident that the imperial center of society would ultimately shift westward and that even the seat of government would move from London to America. The implication of *this train of thought* was that the colonists for their own good needed to stay well informed about the economic details of the empire and about the prevailing state of thinking in Britain about economic policies.

> (Crauford D. Goodison and Stephen Meardon, *The Economic Mind in America: Essays in the History of American Economics – Perspectives on the History of Economic Thought*, ed., Malcolm Rutherford, London and New York: Routledge, 1998, 295)

5. The technology that makes virtual communities possible has the potential to bring enormous leverage to ordinary citizens at relatively little cost: intellectual leverage, social leverage, commercial leverage, and, most important, political leverage. But the technology will not in itself fulfil that potential. *This latent technical power* must be used intelligently and deliberately by an informed population. More people must learn about that leverage and learn to use it, while we still have the freedom to do so, if it is to live up to its potential.

> (Howard Rheingold, *The Virtual Community:*
> *Finding Connection in a Computerized World,*
> London: Secker & Warburg, 1994, 275)

6. Polish modernism uniquely fused constructivism with Dada-surrealism, a vividly internationalist blend for the beleaguered inter-war years. *This fusion of seemingly opposite artistic direction* had a strongly social caste in an age of post-war rebuilding and industrialization.

> (A.L. Rees, *A History of Experimental Film and*
> *Video,* London: British Film Institute, 1999, 54)

7. A relationship of mutual benefit between members of different species is called mutualism or symbiosis. Members of different species often have much to offer each other because they can bring different "skills" to the partnership. *This kind of fundamental asymmetry* can lead to evolutionarily stable strategies of mutual cooperation.

> (Richard Dawkins, *The Selfish Gene*, Oxford:
> Oxford University Press, 2006 (1989), 181)

8. We cannot say for certain whether we are indeed living in a new age, the culture of narcissism, or simply becoming more aware of a situation that has always been with us. Researchers from a variety of disciplines have wrestled with *this vexing question.*

> (Jeffrey Berman, *Narcissism and the Novel,* New
> York: New York University Press, 1990, 48)

9. We communicate an extraordinary range of meanings just through tone of voice. Listen to yourself talk to listeners – babies, dogs, cats – who can't understand concepts but

who respond to intonation. You are talking a language of pure attitude, of love, reassurance, frustration, fatigue. *This emotional overdubbing* can color any event, make a laughing stock of the most sublime poetry, salvage the most banal cliché.

> (Richard A. Lanham, *Analyzing Prose*, New
> York: Charles Scribner's Sons, 1983, 1)

10. Here is something that the psychologists have so far neglected: the love of ugliness for its own sake, the lust to make the world intolerable. Its habitat is the United States. Out of the melting pot emerges a race which hates beauty as it hates truth. The etiology of *this madness* deserves a great deal more study than it has got. There must be causes behind it. It arises and flourishes in obedience to biological laws and not as a mere act of God. What, precisely, are the terms of those laws? And why do they run stronger in America than elsewhere? Let some honest *Privat Dozent* apply himself to the problem.

> (H. L. Mencken, "The Libido for the Ugly," *A
> Mencken Chrestomathy*, New York: Alfred Knopf,
> 1949 (1962), 576)

Drafts in Progress: Revising Instances of "This"as a Demonstrative Pronoun

The changes below were made by a widely respected professional writer.[24] The revisions for the final essay follow the original sentences as they appeared in his penultimate draft. The italics that I have added indicate the changes that the writer made himself. Ask yourself in each case how each change clarifies the writer's ideas and provides a transition between sentences.

Sentences and Revisions

1. A few decades later, Matthew Arnold was to complain that the English Romantics "did not know enough," that their work was insufficiently part of European literature. That is, he thought them too English. I take *this* as another way of saying that they were not English enough since England itself is always more than just English.

He might just as well have said that they were not English enough since England itself is always more than just English. (*The revision of the sentence eliminates the abstract "this" as well as any need to supply a specific clarifying phrase to explain it.*)

2. What Housman's remark reveals is really a fear that we are losing our "Englishness" and are anxious to preserve it before it rots. *This* reminds me of a remark that Edward Thomas, who never pretended to have England in his pocket, made about Rupert Brooke, who did: "The worst of the poetry being written today is that it is too deliberately, and not inevitably, English."

Edward Thomas, who never pretended to have England in his pocket, said of Rupert Brooke, who did, that "[t]he worst of the poetry being written today is that it is too deliberately, and not inevitably, English." (*The revision again changes the syntax of the sentence to avoid any unclear use of "this" on its own.*)

3. Brooke's "The Soldier" is a good example: the thought of England helps him to feel a finer person but he is actually being an emotional parasite and England is simply his host. *This* is understandable in war-time though it has little to do with poetry and it has serious consequences.

This reaction is understandable in war-time though it has little to do with poetry and it has serious consequences. (*The revision clarifies "this" as "This reaction."*)

4. Nationhood becomes harnessed to our ego. Milton appeals to *this* in Areopagitica when he seeks to make his readers feel "noble and puissant" like their country.

Milton appeals to *such a response* in *Areopagitica* when he seeks to make his readers feel "noble and puissant" like their country. (*The unclear "this" becomes "such a response" in the revision, the writer choosing to vary his phrasing.*)

5. An insecurity lurks within all patriotism. *This* is why we make fun of cherished institutions like the Monarchy or the English cricket team: we know they can stand criticism.

> *Thus, we make fun* of cherished institutions like ... *(The revision strengthens the verb by changing it from "is" to "make" as it eliminates the ambiguity of "this" by replacing it with a clear transitional device.)*

6. I can't myself believe that Larkin [the poet Philip Larkin] cared as passionately about guildhalls and carved choirs as these lines make out. It certainly doesn't occur to him that he has any responsibility for England's decline or should be doing anything to stop it. All *this* concerns how the English see themselves, all that many English politicians seem to think about.

> *All these feelings reflect* how the English see themselves, all that some English politicians seem to think about. *(The revision clarifies that the original unclear "this" referred to "feelings.")*

7. What earlier poets found in European poetry was a basis for comparison, a means of testing their own language. *This* opened out their "Englishness" into a realm of moral and artistic choice.

> *Doing so* opened out their "Englishness" into a realm of moral and artistic choice. *(The revision corrects lack of clarity by revealing that "this" referred to the action of poets finding a basis for comparison in European poetry.)*

8. Thus, "every critic should try and possess one great literature, at least, besides his own; and the more unlike his own, the better." *This* is no mere aesthetic tourism, such as we have in plenty ourselves. [The quotation comes from Matthew Arnold, the nineteenth-century English poet and cultural critic.]

> *This aspiration entails* more than mere aesthetic tourism, such as we have in plenty ourselves. *(Here the writer has not only clarified his reference for*

> *"this" but also provided a more specific verb –*
> *"entails" – to replace the simple "is." Anytime you*
> *can substitute an active, specific verb for one of the*
> *forms of the verb "to be" – "is," "was," "will be,"*
> *etc. – you should probably do so.)*

9. Reading such writers may not safeguard us against provinciality but it can help us to see ourselves better for what we are by reminding us of what we are not. At one time it looked as if [Ezra] Pound and [T.S.] Eliot might rectify *this*.

> At one time it looked as if Pound and Eliot might
> *curb our insularity.* (*The change here not only*
> *identifies reference for "this" but enhances the*
> *quality of the verb.*)

10. Even the staunchly English [D.H.] Lawrence turned eagerly to the continent. All *this* was intrinsic to the revolt against Victorianism.

> *A certain cosmopolitanism* was intrinsic to the
> revolt against Victorianism. (*The revision exposes*
> *the untold reference of the original "this": "a certain*
> *cosmopolitanism."*)

11. We still nurture and flaunt a defensive nostalgia that, despite the watershed of the sixties, remains much the same as Larkin's. Indeed, the more embroiled we get in Europe, the stronger such feelings seem to become. Indeed, it is *this* and not just the general negative point itself, which makes me turn now to the poet who does begin to fulfill Arnold's prescriptions for English poetry – Geoffrey Hill.

> Indeed, it is *this resistance* and not just the general
> negative point itself, which makes me turn now to
> the poet who does begin to fulfill Arnold's
> prescriptions for English poetry – Geoffrey Hill. (*The*
> *abstract idea that is implied by the first two*
> *sentences and to which the original "this"*
> *implicitly referred turns out to be "resistence."*)

12. Hill has none of the charm of [Irish poet] Seamus Heaney and his poetry is too cryptic, allusive and plain "difficult" to suit tastes formed by the "poetry circuit." *This* enables him to be pigeon-holed as a poet for academics.

> *It is therefore easy* to pigeon-hole him as a poet for academics. *(Another revision might simply have been "These demanding qualities enable him to be pigeon-holed as a poet for academics.")*

13. *Mercian Hymns* is one of our most searching explorations of the English identity. Yet in Hill *this* goes hand in hand with a twin preoccupation with Europe, though not just with Europe as foreign but with Europe as an essential element in the experience of being English.

> Yet in Hill *this search* goes hand in hand with a twin preoccupation with Europe, though not just with Europe as foreign but with Europe as an essential element in the experience of being English. *(The clarification of "this" involves the easy insertion of a polyptoton – "search" as a noun – that links up neatly with "searching" as an adjective in the previous sentence – "searching explorations." And you thought this – "achievement of coherence" – was hard?)*

14. Moreover, by seeing the war through the eyes of a French poet, Hill makes it clear that World War I was a European war and not just an English one. *This* is something that comes through only fitfully in the poetry of the War Poets themselves.

> *One glimpses this fact* only fitfully in the poetry of the War Poets themselves. *(The revision provides agency for the action implied by the original "this" but left unclear.)*

15. These poets inhabit a larger world than [the English poet A.E.] Housman did. *This* is what makes possible something more than the mere vacationist's poem about Europe that reinforces the distinction between the Europe we visit and the Europe we live in.

They make it possible for other poets to write something more than the mere vacationist's poem about Europe that reinforces the distinction between the Europe we visit and the Europe we live in. *(The elimination of "this" in this instance allows for the simple use of the pronoun "They" which refers to "These poets" in the previous line. The sentences then become more parallel, too.)*

16. The more contemporary we think ourselves, the more Hill will seem old-fashioned. Yet in many ways *this* confirms one's sense of him as a European poet, one who, just like Virgil and Goethe, can distinguish the essential from the ephemeral.

    Yet in many ways *his apparent pedantry* confirms one's sense of him as a European poet, one who, just like Virgil and Goethe, can distinguish the essential from the ephemeral. *(I wonder if you would have guessed that the phrase added in the revision was the one you were meant to infer from the original "this.")*

17. England is something that, in [William] Wordsworth's phrase, we "half-create and half-perceive." Failing *this*, we are left with little but pictures, private versions of a public world.

    But for *this potential*, we would be left with little but pictures, private versions of a public world. *(The revision entails the simple but useful addition of "potential" as reference of the unclear "this.")*

18. Tradition entails the suffering and labor of "common" people as well as artists and statesmen. *This* is where Hill's view of it goes further than Eliot's.

    In this respect, Hill's view of it goes further than Eliot's. *(This simple change suggests that we should try to avoid phrases such as "This is where" or "This is when" or "This is how.")*

19. Thus we find a constant tension in Hill's poems between hints of grace and passages of unflinching tragic realism. It

is too soon to judge how well Hill brings off *this heady combination,* but clear enough that his England and his Europe are both completely impregnated in Christianity. If *this* seems off-putting one might add that, given their history, they are bound to be. To deny it would be an evasion.

> It is too soon to judge how well Hill brings *off this heady combination,* but clear enough that his England and his Europe are both completely impregnated in Christianity. If *this emphasis* seems off-putting to some readers one might add that, given their history, they are bound to be. To deny it would be an evasion. *(The clarification of the use of "this" as a demonstrative pronoun in the second instance rather than its use as a demonstrative adjective in the first illustrates the advantage of the latter.)*

20. *Mercian Hymns* and *Tenebrae* construct their idea of England from specific past lives but in *Canaan England* is seen more frontally, almost as if it were an abstract idea of itself, a character. *This* seems to me characteristic of the expatriate and I can't help remarking that most of the poems in this book have been written since Hill went to work in Boston in 1988.

> *This perspective* seems to me characteristic of the expatriate and I can't help remarking that most of the poems in this book have been written since Hill went to work in Boston in 1988. *(Another simple but effective transformation of a demonstrative pronoun to a demonstrative adjective.)*

21. Hill's own approach may be very different but I believe he shares Lawrence's refusal to re-tell a tale that has already been told in the same terms. *This* is why *Canaan* is important.

> *It is for this reason that Canaan* is important. *(Slight change of syntax to provide the noun – "reason" — to which the original demonstrative pronoun implicitly referred.)*

EXERCISE 6j: Using "This" with a Clarifying Phrase

1. Return to your argumentative draft and identify any instances where you have used "this" without a clarifying phrase. Devise the most appropriate clarifying phrase to articulate the idea to which your original uses of "this" refer.

2. Use "this" with a clarifying phrase in ten groups of sentences. Experiment with a variety of potential clarifying phrases so you can see what a difference a clear phrase can make for your reader.

Keeping a Log

One of the best ways to improve your paragraphing is to read more good paragraphs more closely. So, as you read for your assignments or for pleasure, get into the habit of noticing examples of good – and bad – paragraphs. Note their structures. Consider how their writers have used transitional devices. Explain to yourself how they relate to each other, how they hang together, so to speak.

Below is a page you can use as a log. You may want to use it or something similar to keep a record of examples of good paragraphs as you discover them. You can list the name of the author and title of the book along with the publisher, place and date of publication, and the page on which you have found the exemplary paragraph (in this way you will also gain practice working with the bibliographical material). Give the date on which you first read the paragraph. And, in a separate space, either in your computer or in a writing book, you may even want to identify specific instances of good transitional devices of all types. Whatever you choose to record, try to explain to yourself exactly what principles of connection and generation lie behind the writers' use of these devices and paragraph development.

Author of paragraph	Title	Publisher	Place/date of publication	Page reference	Date para was found

EXERCISE 6k: Paragraphs to Imitate

1. Below are paragraphs for you to imitate. Most were written by professional writers. The content of the paragraphs covers a range of subject areas, and not all of the examples come from essays. (I have chosen examples from a range of types of prose writing, and I have revised some of them slightly to accentuate some of the elements we have discussed in this chapter.)

2. Start by reading some, if not all, of the paragraphs. Then pick five or so and circle all of the rhetorical elements that you think make each paragraph effective.

3. Consider their purposes.

4. Next choose one paragraph, preferably from one of the subject areas you are studying or that you particularly enjoy, and imitate it by following the steps below. (That way, you may gain some knowledge and understanding at the same time that you improve your writing.)

5. As with all of the exercises in this book, only work on your imitation exercises when you are relatively fresh and only for as long as you can really concentrate. But be prepared to repeat them a few times. Repetition is not only a quality of good writing. It is essential for anyone trying to improve his writing. Good luck.

Imitation Steps to Follow

1. Read all of the paragraphs below carefully, noting their structures and employment of transitional devices.

2. Choose one paragraph to imitate and copy it exactly as it is, word for word.

3. Check your result.

4. After a short break, imitate the paragraph once again exactly as it is, only this time try without looking at the example.

5. Check your results again. This time see where your own style has crept into your paragraph and distorted the original.

Make a note of the tendencies that seem to characterize your style, including favorite words and phrases.

6. After another break, imitate the paragraph again, this time writing about a topic that interests you or that you have been assigned. Do not worry about copying the paragraph exactly. Try instead to imitate the general structure and style of the example, duplicating the progression of sentences and their relationship, and incorporating as many of the writer's transitional devices as you can.

7. Check your results once again. As before, note where your imitation departs noticeably from the original. Ask yourself what differences, if any, your departures make to the coherence and success of your paragraph.

8. Repeat step 7 with the same paragraph if you want, but perhaps with a different topic.

9. Repeat all of the steps on another day with another example. If you really want to become a good writer, repeat these steps with another example as often as you can.

Paragraphs to Imitate

1. On a personal level, there is the same dispossession. Valeria, for example, has lost her early political hopes, her government job, her standing in society, her husband, her daughter, and now her ability to speak or to move; finally she confronts, with full awareness, the loss of her life. Minna is about to lose her mother, Gigi her sister. Back in Chicago, Ricky Lester has lost his life and his wife her husband. Even Dewey Spangler, following surgery, is forced to take a forward look to his own dissolution and Corde's cousin, Max Detillion, is moving down the same track, facing "neither virus nor bacteria, but erotic collapse." (71) In addition, Dewey makes Corde aware of his own accumulated losses: the early promise only partly fulfilled, the brilliant career he might have had. Even the Chicago in which they grew up has vanished under the polished grandeur of the present, and the youthful Dewey has also gone: "since then each of them had died at least three or four times." (122)

> (Martin Corner, "The Novel and Public
> Truth: Saul Bellow's The Dean's December"

in *Studies in American Fiction*, 28, no. 1
(Spring 2000), 116-7)

2. [Everything] changed very much during the decade of the thirties. The Great Depression brought production to a very low level. Between 1929 and 1933 the gross output of the private economy dropped by between a third and a half. The sheer magnitude of this movement focused attention, as never before, on movements in the total output of the economy and on their far-reaching consequences for economic and political fortune. Characteristically, to increase production was less central to men's thoughts than to reduce unemployment. "Our primary task is to put people back to work," [American President Franklin D.] Roosevelt said in his first inaugural. But whether directly or as a by-product of the effort to reduce economic insecurity, expanded production began to acquire a growing significance to political liberalism in its American sense.

(John Kenneth Galbraith, *The Affluent Society*,
Boston: Mentor Books, 1971, 151)

3. In Willa Cather's novel *My Antonia*, readers can only speculate on the reasons that Jim does not marry Antonia. Jim may refuse to marry a socially and sexually disgraced woman, or he may desire to pursue a successful career. Or he may simply fear sex and sexuality. But one crucial reason seems clear. Jim does not choose to marry his childhood friend because he refuses to grow up and to face the complexities of adult life: "I wished I could be a little boy again," he tells Antonia. He longs to keep Antonia insulated from time and reality by creating the perfect image of her in his mind, even if maintaining that image means leaving her to her hardships with an empty promise to return soon.

(Kingston University undergraduate
student)

4. The philosophy of experience is known as empiricism. Empiricism says that a concept is valid only if it is derived from, or is testable by, experience. The alternative theory is "rationalism," the view that truth cannot be attained otherwise than by reasoning from self-evident first principles. The rationalist paradigm of knowledge is logic. The empiricist paradigm is science. Empirical knowledge is less certain than logic; it is tentative, responsive to new evidence

and better research, always open to test. It is therefore the very embodiment of the spirit of preparedness to learn. Outside the formal disciplines of logic and mathematics there are no absolute certainties – except of course in religion, which abounds in them, to the extent that people commit murder for their sake. But the experience of history always shows a danger of dogma. What additional bitterness of experience is needed before we learn to return dogma to the kennels of history whence it came?

(A.C. Grayling, *The Reason of Things: Living with Philosophy*, London: Phoenix, 2002, 159)

5. The method of textual interpretation gives the interpreter a certain leeway. He can choose and emphasize as he pleases. It must naturally be possible to find what he claims in the text. My interpretations are no doubt guided by specific purpose. Yet this purpose assumed form only as I went along, playing as it were with my texts, and for long stretches of my way I have been guided only by the texts themselves. Furthermore, the great majority of the texts were chosen at random, on the basis of accidental acquaintance and personal preference rather than in the view of a definite purpose. Studies of this kind do not deal with laws but with trends and tendencies, which cross and complement one another in the most varied ways. I was by no means interested merely in presenting what would serve my purpose in the narrowest sense; on the contrary, it was my endeavor to accommodate multiplex data and to make my formulations correspondingly elastic.

(Erich Auerback, *Mimesis: The Representation of Reality in Western Literature*, Translated by Willard R. Trask, Princeton: Princeton University Press, 1991 (1953), 556)

6. Competing in the knowledge era will present us with large challenges. Life will be more volatile and insecure. Skills and technologies, careers and jobs will change more frequently. We will face ethical dilemmas, particularly over how new knowledge, especially from genetics, should be exploited. Learning and entrepreneurship will be of equal importance. Our national identities and cultures will be challenged. The most dynamic economies will have cultures open to new people and new ideas, which have global horizons. They will not be closed to the world but at ease with diversity and

experimentation. The knowledge-driven economy will require a new raft of economic policies, covering everything from intellectual property rights to investment in science and innovation. Our institutions, public and private, will all have to change quite fundamentally for us to release the potential of the knowledge-driven economy.

(Charles Ledbetter, *Living on Thin Air:
The New Economy*, London: Viking, 1999, 52)

7. I propose an alternative goal for prose stylists: not clarity, but a self-conscious pleasure in words. Such self-consciousness is the only stylistic attitude likely to last beyond the classroom. The only prose didacticism likely to work in America is auto-didacticism and the only possible basis for such teaching is an acute awareness of stylistic surface. Everything in a composition module should be directed toward such an aim. Not clarity but attention must come first. Only such a theory will compensate for the literary tradition that even literate Americans do not possess. Only such an emphasis will aerate the vacuum of stylelessness into which prose style teaching evaporates, will provide the reinforcement that society fails to offer. Only such self-consciousness will equip Americans to cope with the verbiage that surrounds them, to banquet off the nonsense.

(Richard A. Lanham, *Style: An Anti-Textbook*,
New Haven and London: Yale University
Press, 1974, 18-19)

8. A sustainable world would need rules, laws, standards, boundaries, social agreements, and social constraints, of course, as does every human culture. Some of the rules for sustainability would be different from the rules people are used to now. Some of the necessary controls are already coming into being as, for example, in the international ozone agreement and the greenhouse gas negotiations. But rules for sustainability, like every workable social rule, would be put in place not to destroy freedoms, but to create freedoms or to protect them. A ban on bank robbing inhibits the freedom of the thief in order to assure that everyone else has the freedom to deposit and withdraw money safely. A ban on overuse of unrenewable resources or on the generation of a dangerous pollutant protects vital freedom in a similar way.

(Donella Meadows, Jorgen Randers, Dennis
Meadows, *Limits to Growth*, London and
Stirling, VA: Earthscan, 2006, 257)

9. The love of flowers is instinct in mankind. It makes itself
apparent in the earliest days of childhood when the height of
ambition is reached if one may become the sole processor, the
guardian and the tiller of even the smallest plot of ground. It
is, likely enough, a very modest piece of Mother Earth,
chosen because it is situated in an out-of-the-way corner and
possibly out of sight. But it is your undisputed property, and
you are left to follow your own devices: to dig, to sow, to
tend and to gather the produce – if there be any – how and
when you yourself shall determine. The youthful owner
becomes, unconsciously, a philosopher. It is the sense of
ownership which appeals most strongly to his untutored and
undisciplined nature. The quest of the beautiful, the desire to
excel in the art of gardening, the determination to induce the
soil to yield its richest treasures at his behest are a later
development of his maturer years. But the consciousness of
ownership and the desire for pleasure are among the earliest
characteristics of childhood, and so sure a foothold do they
obtain that the onward march of after years neither
obliterates nor eradicates them.

(F. Hadfield Farthing, F.R.H.S., *Saturday in
my Garden*, London: Grant Richards, Ltd.,
1911, 15)

10. A recurring debate among historians concerns the role of
great men in history as compared with the role played by
underlying forces, whether of the random actions of individuals or of class and economic factors. As with so many
arguments of this kind, these debates could hardly continue
unless there were good points to be said on each side. But
from one intellectual or cultural climate to another the
emphasis varies greatly. In cricket, for example, the role of
the captain has been consistently underrated in recent years.
This tendency should hardly surprise us, however. We have
been living in an era in which the measurable has
increasingly become the predominant mode of valuation.
Hence the obsession we see with targets and costs and, for
example, in teaching with the increasing number of tests to be
taken and marked.

(Mike Brearley, "Captains Courageous Wage
War of Wits," *the Guardian,* June, 2004)

11. Slavery was a fact of life in nineteenth-century Africa, and the explorers came to terms with it in different ways. Fundamentally their attitude was ambivalent. On the one hand, they hated the "peculiar institution" and used it as unique evidence that Africa was a benighted country, in need of deliverance by European capital, institutions and religion. On the other hand, it was something which they could at the very least coexist with in their daily lives, and it was often something from which they could derive considerable advantage. This ambivalence in the explorers' attitude was made more complex by a fundamental ambiguity within slavery itself. African slavery was subdivided into domestic thralldom and the trade in human flesh for export. These two divisions were as distinct as the Papal Inquisition and the much more sinister Spanish Inquisition, yet were often confused, sometimes by the explorers themselves. They are one of the sources of the many conflicting reports on African slavery. The different accounts by the explorers reflect a differential experience of domestic slavery and slavery for export.

(Frank McLynn, *Hearts of Darkness:
The European Exploration of Africa,* London:
Hutchinson, 1992, 189)

12. Throughout the nineteenth century the True, the Good, and the Beautiful preserved their precarious existence in the minds of earnest atheists. But their very earnestness was their undoing since it made it impossible for them to stop at a half-way house. Pragmatists explained that Truth is what it pays to believe. Historians of morals reduced the Good to a matter of tribal custom. Beauty was abolished by the artists in a revolt against the sugary insipidities of a philistine epoch and in a mood of fury in which satisfaction is to be derived only from what hurts. And so the world was swept clear not only of God as a person but of God's essence as an ideal to which man owed an ideal allegiance, while the individual, as a result of a crude and uncritical interpretation of sound doctrines, was left without any inner defence against social pressure.

(Bertrand Russell, "On Being Modern-Minded," *Unpopular Essays*, London: George Allen and Unwin Ltd., 92-3)

13. To the biologist the problem of socialism appears largely as a problem of size. The extreme socialists desire to run every nation as a single business concern. I do not suppose that Henry Ford would find much difficulty running Andorra or Luxembourg on a socialist basis. He has already more men on his pay-roll than their population. It is conceivable that a syndicate of Fords, if we could find them, would make Belgium Ltd or Denmark Inc. pay their way. But while nationalization of certain industries is an obvious possibility in the largest of states, I find it no easier to picture a completely socialized British Empire or United States than an elephant turning somersaults or a hippopotamus jumping a hedge.

(J.B.S. Haldane, "On Being the Right Size," *Possible Worlds and Other Essays*, London: Chatto and Windus, 1927, reprinted 1930, 26)

14. The time has come to realize that the interracial drama acted out on the American continent has not only created a new black man, it has created a new white man, too. No road whatever will lead Americans back to the simplicity of this European village where white men still have the luxury of looking on me as a stranger. I am not, really, a stranger any longer for any American alive. One of the things that distinguishes Americans from other people is that no other people has ever been so deeply involved in the lives of black men, and vice versa. This fact faced, with all its implications, it can be seen that the history of the American Negro problem is not merely shameful; it has also something of an achievement. For even when the worst has been said, it must also be added that the perpetual change posed by his problem was always, somehow, perpetually met. It is precisely this black-white experience which may prove of indispensable value to us in the world we face today. This world is white no longer, and it will never be white again.

(James Baldwin, "Stranger in the Village," *Collected Essays*, New York, N.Y.: The Library of America, 1998, 129)

15. The paragraph has a dual character: it is an essay in miniature, endowed with some measure of individuality, composed of related material, and as carefully designed as the essay itself; but it is also an integral part of the composition in which it stands. Hence, the paragraph cannot be fully studied without reference to the whole essay. Nevertheless, it will be necessary to concentrate attention on the paragraph as an independent unit if we are to understand the mechanics of its construction. As it happens, the two areas of discussion overlap. For example, the principles of completeness, limitation, and division, which, as we have seen, regulate the proper disposition of an argument during the planning stage of an essay, are equally relevant to a just ordering of material in the paragraph.

> (Robin S. Harris and Robert L. McDougall,
> *The Undergraduate Essay*, Toronto: University
> of Toronto Press, 1964 (1958), 57)

16. Homo sapiens is indeed an unprecedented animal, with many unique or extreme traits. Humans achieve their goals by complex chains of behaviour, assembled on the spot and tailored to the situation. They plan the behaviour using cognitive models of the causal structures of the world. They learn these models in their lifetimes and communicate them through language, which allows the knowledge to accumulate within a group and over generations. They manufacture and depend upon many kinds of tools. They exchange goods and favour over long periods of time. Food is transported long distances, processed extensively, stored, and shared. Labour is divided between the sexes. Humans form large, structured coalitions, especially among males, and coalitions wage war against each other. Humans use fire. Kinship systems are complex and vary with other aspects of their lifestyles. Mating relations are negotiated by kin, often by groups exchanging daughters. Ovulation is concealed, and females may choose to have sex at any time rather than at certain points in a reproductive cycle.

> (Steven Pinker, *How the Mind Works*,
> London: Allen Lane, 1999, 186)

17. The political critique of beauty is composed of two distinct arguments. The first urges that beauty, by preoccupying our attention, distracts attention from wrong social arrangements.

It makes us inattentive, and therefore eventually indifferent, to the project of bringing about arrangements that are just. The second argument holds that when we stare at something beautiful, make it an object of sustained regard, our art is destructive to the object. This argument is most often prompted when the gaze is directed toward a human face or form, but the case presumably applies equally when the beautiful thing is a mourning dove, or a trellis spilling over with sweet pea, or a book whose pages are being folded back for the first time. The complaint has given rise to the generalized discrediting of the act of "looking," which is charged with "reifying" the very object that appears to be the subject of admiration.

(Elaine Scarry, *On Beauty and Being Just*,
London: Duckworth, 2006, 58)

18. Some people dislike the word *argument* because it sounds too pugnacious. But it is a civilized term; we make arguments instead of war. We persuade people rather than beat them into submission. Democracy depends on argument. Candidates argue that they are more qualified than their opponents; representatives argue that their policies are better than the alternatives. Lawyers and judges argue about what the laws mean. Citizens argue with each other about what's right or wrong with society. In tyrannies, people don't argue–at least not in public. Democracy is unending disputation.

(Richard Marius, *A Writer's Companion*, 3rd
ed., New York: Alfred A. Knopf, 1991, 61)

19. Research on writing practice has shown that good writers do not create wonderful texts in one smooth step. Rather, writers plan, compose, revise, throw drafts away, rewrite, and sometimes seem to do nothing at all. These processes do not simply involve expression. People express ideas in writing, but they also react to their texts. Writers read and critique their texts. They talk to themselves about ways to improve their writing. One question in studies of the creative process is "How conscious is the creative process?" The related question for studying production processes like writing is "Does it make sense to guide students in monitoring their thought processes as they write and revise?"

(Collete Dalute, "Do Writers Talk to
Themselves?,"*The Acquisition of Written*

> *Language: Response and Revision*, ed. Sarah
> Warshauer Freedman, Norwood, N.J: Ablex
> Publishing Corporation, 1985, 133)

20. Moral hazard is an inevitable problem in the real economy. While it is impossible for insurance companies (or anyone else) to avoid moral hazard altogether, they can take steps to reduce it. For example, they do not offer insurance against being fired or becoming pregnant, which is a shame, because it would be great to have that kind of insurance. The reason is easy to see: it is easy to arrange to be fired or to get pregnant. There are many people who would like to leave their jobs and many others who would like to have children, and such people would be particularly eager to buy an insurance policy that would pay them handsomely for putting their plans into action. As a result, moral hazard destroys the market for private unemployment insurance.

> (Tim Harford, *The Undercover Economist*,
> London: Abacus, 2007, 126)

Current Stages in Our Writing Process for Argumentative Essays

1. **The Procrastination Stage:** Incorporate whatever form of procrastination puts you in the right frame of mind to begin writing.

2. **The Freewriting Stage:** Set aside around 30 minutes and write with abandon about your topic. Then take a break.

3. **The Planning Stage:** Reread your freewriting and then organize the ideas, trying not to become too attached to your plan.

4. **The Mastermind Stage:** Compose a mastermind draft, writing or typing yourself to a conclusion.

5. **The Argumentative or Persuasive Stage:** Copy the conclusion at the end of your mastermind draft and paste it at the beginning.

6. **The Weighty Stage – Thesis Statements:** Revise your newly pasted conclusion into a more effective thesis.

7. **The Content Stage – Paragraphing:** Once you have swapped roles and read your argumentative draft for the first time, make sure that you take plenty of time to substantiate and refine the content of your essays. You may need to consider rearranging the order of your paragraphs since normally it is best to structure ideas from the least to the most important or from the most general to the most specific. You may also need to make short paragraphs longer by specifying, explaining, and / or reiterating central claims or to generate new paragraphs from overly general sentences in paragraphs that are too long. In either case, ensure that you make your sentences and paragraphs – and hence your draft – as coherent as you can. In other words, add explicit transitional devices where necessary and include a clarifying phrase wherever you may have used "this" as a demonstrative pronoun. Finally, check your style so you express yourself as clearly and stylishly as possible.

CHAPTER 4

The Stylish Stage: Formal Introductory Paragraphs

If thesis statements exemplify one side of the paradox that sometimes distinguishes the drafting and writing of our argumentative essays (what may look easy proves difficult), then formal introductory paragraphs probably represent the other (what may look difficult proves easy). For, in the abstract, writing a good introduction probably seems more challenging and certainly more demanding than writing a simple declarative sentence. But an opening paragraph is, after all, just another paragraph. It shares the same traits of a good paragraph that appear elsewhere in the body of your essay, and, once you've begun to master the principles behind generating well-developed paragraphs, writing effective – even stylish – opening paragraphs can be invitingly simple.

For all of their similarities to regular paragraphs, however, formal introductory paragraphs are unique, given their location in your essays. Due to these differences, rhetoricians have placed formal introductory paragraphs in a special category. This classification into five types has made them easy to distinguish and relatively simple to learn to write, at least once you know what you are hoping to achieve and the nature of the context that each type of formal introductory paragraphs provides. For the qualities that characterize the five types of formal introductory paragraphs have emerged over time following sustained observation and the documentation of the natural practices upon which successful writers and speakers have relied. Consequently, none ought to seem forced, and none, despite my reference, will, I think, strike you as particularly "formal." They should seem quite natural and, dare I say it, commonsensical, especially the four on which we will concentrate the most. That's the beauty of our paradox.

The First as Last and the Last as First

The paradox of your formal introductory paragraphs applies also to the timing of their final composition, the moment in your process at which you are most likely to place them into your essays. You should usually start your essays with formal introductory paragraphs, but many times they may be one of the last, if not the last, part of your essays that you write. Before then, you will have generated your thesis through your mastermind draft and placed it at the start of the first draft of your argumentative essay. You will have read and reread that draft, revising it in the light of your questioning of it as editor so that you know more confidently what your argument is and how you have arrived at it. You may even have refined your thesis for the final time.

Yet, in the process, you will have left yourself conspicuously short of any suitable beginning for your essay. As a consequence, the essay will almost seem to start too abruptly. So you will want to add the final, stylish touch to your draft: a perfectly chosen formal introductory paragraph. This paragraph should always replace any mapping paragraph you may have used as part of your planning stage and your mastermind draft. It should be proportionate in length to the overall length of your argumentative essay (which usually means approximately ten percent of the length of the essay as a whole or around six or eight sentences, although you will eventually have to trust your own judgment). And it should inform and engage your reader, leading her seamlessly to your thesis and the evidence that supports it.

Types of Formal Introductory Paragraphs

1. **Introduction Narrative** provides a short narrative related to your thesis or uses an anecdote to provide a context for your central argument.
2. **Introduction Preparatory** gives background knowledge or information that situates your thesis in a useful context and ensures that your readers can understand that context well enough to follow your argument and to judge its validity.

3. **Introduction Corrective** expresses a widely accepted opinion about your theme and then proposes an alternative as if to correct it, possibly also suggesting how your thesis may have been misunderstood or overlooked.

4. **Introduction Inquisitive** asks key questions, almost always more than one but usually fewer than five, which relate both to your thesis and to each other.

5. **Introduction Paradoxical** explains why your thesis is valid even if it seems at first unlikely or inconceivable.

Sample Introductory Paragraphs

As with any rhetorical device, it's imperative to know what qualities you are trying to emulate and what effects you are aiming for when you use formal introductory paragraphs. The following edited models provide classic examples of our five types of formal introductory paragraphs. Corbett first selected them as examples and identified them as I have below in his *Classical Rhetoric for the Modern Student*, perhaps the most authoritative text on rhetoric written last century.[25] All were written by professional writers.

1. Narrative

A light flashed on the central switchboard of the New York Telephone Company office in Forest Avenue early Sunday morning. One of the operators on duty plugged in on the line. She heard the sound of heavy breathing. "Hello," she said, "hello." There was no answer, just that heavy breathing sound. She turned to another operator and asked her to trace the call. This operator quickly found that it was coming from a house nearby. Then she cut in on the line, holding it open, while the first operator notified the police that something appeared to be wrong. Then a woman gasped: "I've been stabbed." The operator immediately cut the police in on the conversation, and both she and the desk officer heard the woman repeat: "I've been stabbed. I've been attacked with a knife." A second later, the voice added: "My husband has been stabbed, too."

Then there was silence. It lasted only a second. Then a new voice, a little boy's voice, came on the wire.

"My mother is bleeding," the voice said.

Mrs. Thompson told the boy police already were on the way.

"I'll wait for the police outside," he said.

"No," she told him, "you better stay with your mother."

Such was the beginning of a drama that was to shock the nation.[26]

The example above does not come from a conventional argumentative essay, and it is probably longer than most of the formal narrative openings that you will write. It may also include more detailed dialogue. But I suspect you can see from it two main qualities that you ought to strive for fundamentally with a narrative introductory paragraph. Such an opening should engage your audience, pulling them into your essay. It does not need to be as dramatic as this example or fictional. It may certainly be autobiographical, and, in my view, you may write your formal narrative introductions from the first person singular (which means you can use the 'I' word), assuming, that is, that your individual lecturer or instructor does not mind.

Overall, in fact, you may construct narrative for this type of formal introductory paragraph in a host of ways. In addition to being fictional narratives or autobiographical ones, narrative introductions may take the form of general historical narratives (retelling an incident in history) or narratives about others you know. They may take the form of a simple moral tale. Indeed, they may take the form of any type of illustrative story that chronicles events, lessons, or insights that lead clearly to an expression of your thesis and its support in the body of your essays. As a result, narrative introductory paragraphs should be relatively easy to understand. The best ones, however, will require some thought, for they should at least hint at the slant or point of view that you will take with respect to your thesis statement. And, ideally, they will be clearly pertinent to your central argument. (Our chapter on thesis statements will have taught you the final sentence in this example would have to be more specific to achieve this aim.)

2. Preparatory

> Beginnings are apt to be shadowy, and so it is with the beginnings of that great mother of life, the sea. Many people have debated how and when the earth got its oceans, and it is not surprising that their explanations do not always agree. For the plain and inescapable truth is that no one was there to see, and in the absence of eye-witness accounts there is bound to be a certain amount of disagreement. So if I tell here the story of how the young planet Earth acquired an ocean, it must be a story pieced together from many sources and containing many whole chapters the details of which we can only imagine.[27]

Preparatory introductions are probably the most frequently used formal introductory paragraphs, and you can most likely understand why. As in the example from Rachel Carson above, preparatory openings provide a context through which you can expect your readers to understand the topic that your essay addresses well enough to follow your argument. Preparatory introductions, therefore, are essentially discursive rather than narrative, factual rather than fictional or personal, and this example is probably just about the length that you might use in your essays. Yet it also demonstrates that preparatory introductory paragraphs can set out the main positions and counter positions that mark the debates surrounding your topic and thesis. In either case, as its name implies, a good preparatory introduction ensures that your readers are sufficiently *prepared* to understand your thesis so they can appreciate the support and evidence that you provide. Preparatory introductions act to establish a context of knowledge sufficient enough to engage the reader with your argument. Here we can understand the way in which this preparatory context leads the reader successfully to the statement of what would seem the potential thesis, signaled clearly with the linking device "So." It thus exemplifies the need to associate your formal introductory paragraphs with your thesis and your thesis to the paragraph that follows.

3. Corrective

Most people who bother with the matter at all would admit that the English language is in a bad way, but it is generally assumed that we cannot by conscious action do anything about it. Our civilization is decadent, and our language – so the argument runs – must inevitably share in the general collapse. It follows that any struggle against the abuse of language is a sentimental archaism, like preferring candles to electric light or hansom cabs to airplanes. Underneath this lies the half-conscious belief that language is a natural growth and not an instrument which we shape for our own purposes.

Now, it is clear that the decline of a language must ultimately have political and economic causes: [for] it is not due simply to the bad influence of this or that individual writer. But an effect can become a cause, reinforcing the original cause and producing the same effect in an intensified form, and so on indefinitely. [For example] [a] man may take to drink because he feels himself to be a failure, and then fail all the more completely because he drinks. It is rather the same thing that is happening to the English language. It becomes ugly and inaccurate because our thoughts are foolish, but the slovenliness of our language makes it easier for us to have foolish thoughts. The point is that the process is reversible. Modern English, especially written English, is full of bad habits which spread by imitation and which can be avoided if one is willing to take the necessary trouble. If one gets rid of these habits one can think more clearly, and to think clearly is a necessary first step toward political regeneration: so that the fight against bad English is not frivolous and is not the exclusive concern of professional writers. I will come back to this presently, and I hope that by that time the meaning of what I have said here will have become clearer. Meanwhile, here are five specimens of the English language as it is now habitually written.[28]

A corrective introductory paragraph represents a slightly more specific type of preparatory introduction. With a corrective introductory paragraph, you will still look to set out a context for your reader that will allow her to appreciate your thesis. But, with this type, your context will take a more particular shape. That is, the corrective targets a particular opinion about your topic that you will seek to refute in your thesis and essay. For this reason, it assumes that your reader will most likely hold this commonly mistaken view about your topic. Thus, it's perhaps the most appropriate choice when you are writing about issues about which there is an existing, well-established opinion.

Like the earlier narrative one, this example is longer than you will typically write (and is actually two paragraphs), but in your shorter corrective introductory paragraphs you will still want to establish the prevailing view clearly for your reader before you state your thesis, as George Orwell does here when he says "Our civilization is decadent and our language – so the argument runs – must inevitably share in the general collapse." You must, however, explain the position you are going to correct well enough so that your reader not only understands the correction herself but also knows that you understand it as well. And, more importantly, you must explain that position clearly enough so that you will stand a good chance of persuading that reader, who, you must think, may hold that prevailing view herself. If you fail to show that level of understanding, your reader will assume you are insufficiently prepared. She may reject you as an authority on your topic. And she almost certainly won't be convinced by your argument about it.

4. Inquisitive

Does history repeat itself? In our Western world in the eighteenth and nineteenth centuries, this question used to be debated as an academic exercise. [That is] [t]he spell of well-being which our civilization was enjoying at the time had dazzled our grandfathers into the quaint pharisaical notion that they were "not as other men are;" they had come to believe that our Western society was exempt from the possibility of falling into those mistakes and mishaps that have been the ruin of certain other civilizations whose history, from beginning to end, is an open book. [Yet] [t]o us, in our generation, the old question has rather suddenly taken on a new and very practical significance. We have awakened to the truth that Western man and his works are no more invulnerable than many extinct civilizations. So today, with some anxiety, we are searching the scriptures of the past to find out whether they contain a lesson that we can decipher. Does history give us any information about our own prospects? And, if it does, what is the burden of it? Does it spell out for us an inexorable doom? Or does it inform us of probabilities of our own future?[29]

As you can see, the inquisitive introductory paragraph poses questions for the reader. It allows you to establish a context for your essay by explicitly framing some or all of the questions that you may have asked yourself or that you assume intelligent readers might themselves ask in response to your topic or your thesis. Here Arnold J. Toynbee articulates one overarching – and potentially profound – question at the start of the paragraph: "Does history repeat itself?" He then explains the context of that question, much as he might in a preparatory or corrective introduction, at a length that is not too much longer than you might sometimes write. Yet, like a good essayist who recognizes the demands of the formal inquisitive opening, Toynbee is not content simply to ask one question, and neither should you be. Once he, like Carson, moves to a thesis-like statement, signaled by the word *So*, he offers four more specific questions for his readers.

We might see these questions as subsets of his first overriding one. With each, Toynbee specifies another line of enquiry related to history's repetitive tendencies (or lack of repetitive tendencies). In this way, he indicates to his readers that he has considered his topic carefully. He presents himself as a thoughtful essayist whose opinion about his issue they can trust. Moreover, in moving from the general to the specific in his introduction, he also clarifies for his readers, in advance, key questions that they can now expect him to answer throughout his essay as part of his argument.

We can therefore take a couple of key points away from this example, whatever your opinion about the initial question. One is that you should normally provide more than one or two questions for your readers in your inquisitive formal introductory paragraphs. In fact, it's probably wise always to try and match Toynbee and provide three, perhaps even four, questions in your inquisitive openings. The second is that you must attempt to make your questions both increasingly specific and pertinent to your thesis (which is itself never a question, remember). You will then prepare your readers for your argument. And they will accept you as an essayist whom they can trust to be even-minded – even if finally they remain unconvinced of your thesis (establishing such trust amounts to half the struggle).

5. Paradoxical

The most characteristic English play on the subject of physical love is Shakespeare's *Antony and Cleopatra*. It is characteristic because it has no love secrets. The English, as their drama represents them, are a nation endlessly communicative about love without ever enjoying it. [As a consequence] [f]ull-blooded physical relationships engaged in with mutual delight are theatrically taboo. [By contrast] [t]hwarted love is preferred, the kind Mr. Coward wrote about in *Brief Encounter*, where two married people form a sad and meagre attachment without being able to follow it through. [Therefore] [a]t the end of the play on some quite different subject – religion, perhaps, or politics – it is customary for the hero to say, as he does in *Robert's Wife*: "I was deeply in love with a fine woman," and for the wife to reply: "My dear, dear husband"; but there should be no hint elsewhere in the text that they have as much as brushed lips.[30]

The paradoxical represents the final type of formal introductory paragraphs. Like the previous four types, the example here provides a context for the topic of his essay. It demonstrates that Kenneth Tynan, one of the most influential theatre critics of the last generation, knows his subject. The difference is that his context focuses not on a prevailing counter opinion but specifically on a defining paradox: that Shakespeare's *Antony and Cleopatra* is the most characteristic English play about physical love precisely because it contains little if any physical love. The point is a subtle and intriguing one, and no doubt admirers of Shakespeare will have an opinion about its veracity.

But not all topics you will be asked to write about will be characterized by their own paradoxes. Even those that are will require a fair amount of specialist knowledge on your part – and the part of your reader – to recognize. So, while I don't want you to think you should stifle your ambitions, for these reasons it's probably best to be cautious when first learning to incorporate formal introductory paragraphs into your essays. It's probably safest to opt for the paradoxical only when you are absolutely sure that your perceived paradox exists. Otherwise you may only succeed in confusing yourself as well as your reader. And you can always rely on one of the other four types of formal introductory paragraphs. One of them will almost always be equally as effective and easier to write.

EXERCISE 7: Imitating Formal Introductory Paragraphs

Below are examples of our four main types of formal introductory paragraphs. In some cases I have revised them slightly to eliminate personal and historical eccentricities of punctuation and spelling and to emphasize clearly some of the key elements of the types.

1. Please read all of the examples carefully and more than once. Like all examples to imitate, these selected texts can teach you something about their subjects as well as about their writers' prose and paragraph styles.
2. Think carefully about which type each example represents and why.
3. Choose one example from each type and imitate it using the same steps of imitation as you used before when imitating the paragraphs in the previous chapter. Some of these imitations may be tricky, but keep at them.
4. Check your attempts/results with a friend or fellow student or your lecturer.
5. Consider the lessons that you have learned and the ways in which formal introductory paragraphs not only add elegance and grace to your essays but also convey important knowledge and understanding to your reader.

Examples of Formal Introductory Paragraphs

Narrative

1. On a winter day some years ago, coming out of Pittsburgh on one of the expresses of the Pennsylvania Railroad, I rolled eastward for an hour through the coal and steel towns of Westmoreland County. It was familiar ground; boy and man, I had been through it often before. But somehow I had never quite sensed its appalling desolation. Here was the very heart of industrial America, the center of its most lucrative and characteristic activity, the boast and pride of the richest and grandest nation ever seen on earth – and here was a scene so dreadfully hideous, so intolerably bleak and forlorn that it reduced the whole aspiration of man to a macabre and depressing joke. Here was wealth beyond computation, almost beyond imagination – and here were human habitations so abominable that they would have disgraced a race of alley cats.

> (H.L. Mencken, "The Libido of the Ugly",
> *A Mencken Chrestomathy*, New York: Alfred A.
> Knopf, 1949, reprinted 1962, 573)

2. There is a spider crawling along the matted floor of the room where I sit. He runs with heedless, hurried haste; he hobbles awkwardly towards me; he stops; he sees the giant shadow before him; and, at a loss whether to retreat or proceed, meditates his huge foe. But as I do not start up and seize upon the straggling caitiff, as he would upon a hapless fly within his toils, he takes heart and ventures on with mingled cunning, impudence and fear. As he passes me, I lift up the matting to assist his escape, glad to get rid of the unwelcome intruder, and shudder at the recollection after he is gone. A child, a woman, a clown, or a moralist a century ago would have crushed the little reptile to death. My philosophy has gone beyond that act. I bear the creature no ill will, but still I hate the very sight of it. The spirit of malevolence survives the practical exertion of it. We learn to curb our will and keep our overt exertion within the bounds of humanity long before we subdue our sentiments and imaginations to the same mild tone. We give up the external demonstration, the *brute*

violence, but cannot part with the essence or principle of hostility. We do not tread upon the poor little animal in question but we regard it with a sort of mystic horror and superstitious loathing. It will ask another hundred years of fine writing and hard thinking to cure us of the prejudice and make us feel towards this ill-omened bribe with something of "the milk of human kindness" instead of their own shyness and venom.

> (William Hazlitt, "On the Pleasure of Hating,"
> *Selected Essays of William Hazlitt 1778-1830*, ed.
> Geoffrey Keynes, London: The Nonesuch Press,
> 1946, 243-4)

3. Years ago, I went to Achill for Easter. I was a student at Trinity then and I had the loan of a friend's cottage. It was a one-storey, stone building with two rooms and a view of sloping fields. April was cold that year. The cottage was in sight of the Atlantic and at night a bitter, humid wind blew across the shore. By day there was heckling sunshine but after dark a fire was necessary. The loneliness of the place suited me. My purposes in being there were purgatorial and I had no intention of going out and about. I had done erratically, to say the least, in my first year exams. In token of the need to do better, I had brought with me a small accusing volume of the Court poets of the silver age. In other words, I had those sixteenth century English songwriters, like Wyatt and Raleigh, whose lines appear so elegant, so off-hand yet whose poems smell of the gallows.

> (Evan Boland, "A Kind of Scar: The Woman
> Poet in a National Tradition," *Nations and
> Identities: Classic Readings*, ed. Vincent P. Pecora,
> Oxford: Blackwell, 2001, 318)

4. I remember attending a workshop at the 1974 NCTE meeting in New Orleans. The crisp teacher who led the session asked us, as you would a class, "What's the first thing you teach when you teach children math?" Addition! "And the second?" Subtraction! "The third?" Multiplication! (We were getting a little bored. But teachers tend to be patient, so we went on to chorus division, geometry, and algebra). "Fine," she said. "Now. What's the first thing you teach when you teach writing?"

The room went off like slow popcorn. I'm sure some fairly strong pockets said, "Reading," "Sentences," "Grammar," and "Letters." I heard a few single voices suggest thesis sentences, spelling, and diagramming. And I am fairly certain that I was not alone in my almost mute and mindless stammer. All the English teachers in the room were certain about the proper sequence of mathematics instruction, but no two agreed on, and most had not before considered, the same progression in English.

> (Susan Miller, "Classical Practice and Contemporary Basics," *The Rhetorical Tradition and Modern Writing*, ed. James J. Murphy, New York: The Modern Language Association of America, 1982, 46)

Preparatory

1. Over the past several years, a change has been taking place in our ideas about language and, as a consequence, about the (literary) work, which owes at least its phenomenal existence to language. This change is obviously linked to current developments in, among other fields, linguistics, anthropology, Marxism, and psychoanalysis. The change affecting the notion of the work does not necessarily come from the internal renewal of each of these disciplines, but proceeds, rather, from their encounter at the level of an object that traditionally depends on none of them. Interdisciplinary activity, valued today as an important aspect of research, cannot be accomplished by simple confrontations between various specialized branches of knowledge. Interdisciplinary work is not a peaceful operation. It begins effectively when the solidarity of the old disciplines breaks down to the benefit of a new object and a new language, neither of which is in the domain of those branches of knowledge that one calmly sought to confront.

   It is precisely this uneasiness with classification that allows for a diagnosis of a certain mutation.

   > (Roland Barthes, "From Work to Text," *Textual Strategies: Perspectives in Post-Structural Criticism*, ed. Josue V. Harari, Ithaca, NY: Cornell UP, 1979, 73)

2. According to many academic studies, the last three decades have seen a large growth in privately owned public areas. The rights of private ownership significantly reduce the ability of the police to enter and search such areas, and, as a result, traditional policing has become less effective. In response, both the police and owners have resorted to applying environmental controls. Perhaps the most controversial of these controls has been the use of surveillance such as CCTV cameras. Other methods include so-called "access control," the attempt to establish a clear distinction between public and private areas, and "territorial reinforcements" that create a common feeling of ownership so individuals carry out their own surveillance out of a sense of pride and collective responsibility. To be as effective as necessary, however, all three methods must be employed alongside traditional policing.

(Adapted from an essay by a Kingston University undergraduate)

3. In the wake of World War II, the unofficial cartoonist laureate of the war, Bill Mauldin, turned the focus of his comic art to life within America's borders. In a 1946 panel, he portrayed two men talking in the shadow of the United States Capitol building. The listener was clearly a slick senator; the speaker looked to be a well-groomed tramp. His question no doubt left the senator fumbling for an answer: "Do you mean your American Way or my American Way, Senator?"

Mauldin did not provide us with the senator's response, but it hardly matters. The tramp's question all but answers itself. The supposed post-war consensus, the shared American Way, had not been achieved by unanimous consent, the tramp was suggesting, but by leaving out those who did not fit in. The popular imagination of America might have attained a single, clean vision of the nation, but only by cropping out anything that could blur the picture. The imagined American Way would not admit it, but there were others trying to climb into the frame.

(Bruce Lenthall, "Outside the Panel – Race in America's Popular Imagination: Comic Strips Before and After World War II," Cambridge: *Journal of American Studies*, 32, 1998, I, 39)

4. As the 20th century drew to a close, we were increasingly likely to encounter the cinema through other media – on television, home video, DVD, or the internet. Media and industry convergences of the late 20th century were enacted in the rise of Home Box Office in the late 1970s, the emergence of home video in the 1980s, and the move from digital special effects to digital editing and projection across the last three decades. Web marketing and access to films online accompanied the rise of corporate conglomerates like *Disney-Capital Cities-ABC* in 1996, and synergetic entities vertically integrated across categories as seemingly disparate as entertainment, information, food and nuclear power, and with a formidable global reach. As *New Economist* editor Frances Cairncross announced, distance is dead in the free-market world where corporations build brave new markets with the dissolution of the nation-state and the wiring of the Third World.

> (Lisa Cartwright, "Film and the digital in visual studies: film studies in the era of convergence," London, Thousand Oaks, CA and New Delhi: *The Journal of Visual Culture*, Vol. I (1), 2002, 7)

Corrective

1. In some ways professions are like people. They are born at certain times in certain circumstances; they go through frequently painful adolescence in which they try to define themselves both for their own sakes and as a way to establish their legitimacy before the general public; and they make choices that significantly affect their entire lives. Once established in their maturity, they put the difficulties and doubts of earlier years behind them and settle into a long period of stability and productivity. Any profession's life span is a capricious thing, however, because it depends on luck, good health, and the length of time that particular profession can serve usefully.

> (Donald C. Stewart, "The Model Teachers and the Harvardization of English Departments," *The Rhetorical Tradition and Modern Writing*, ed. James J. Murphy, New York: The Modern Language Association of America, 1982, 118)

2. Every war is ironic because every war is worse than expected. Every war constitutes an irony of situation because its means are so melodramatically disproportionate to its presumed ends. In the Great War eight million people were destroyed because two persons, the Archduke Francis Ferdinand and his Consort, had been shot. The Second World War offers even more preposterous ironies. Ostensibly begun to guarantee the sovereignty of Poland, that war managed to bring about Poland's bondage and humiliation. Air bombardment, which was supposed to shorten the war, prolonged it by inviting those who were its targets to cast themselves in the role of victim-heroes and thus stiffen their resolve.

   But the Great War was more ironic than any before or since. It was a hideous embarrassment to the prevailing Meliorist myth which had dominated the public consciousness for a century. It reversed the Idea of Progress.

   (Paul Fussell, *The Great War and Modern Memory*, Oxford: Oxford University Press, 1975, 2000, 7-8)

3. We are living in a globalized world. National economies are more open to one another than ever before. International trade is at an unprecedented level, and businesses send huge quantities of capital across national boundaries. Millions of people migrate yearly in search of jobs and better living conditions while corporate executives seem to think nothing about relocating when they are offered better pay and perks. For these reasons many people regard globalization as irreversible, no matter what its consequences. Yet, following the financial crisis of 2008, many commentators now suggest that the globalization of the past forty years has reached its end and that we need to re-think our economic structures and the theories that underpin them.

   (Kingston University undergraduate student)

4. If businessman and philanthropist Scott Griffin committed a misdemeanor as a young boy, he was sent to his room and not allowed out until he had read and remembered some piece of classical poetry. Scott now presides over what is sometimes described as the world's richest poetry award, the Griffin prize, with prize money totaling 200,000

tax-free Canadian dollars. The psychology by which an intended punishment became a lifelong passion might only be explained by close analysis of that particular father and son relationship. But in any event, poetry (or at least a few poets each year) is certainly better off for it. Yet I have also seen the reverse happen. In fact, it's more common that a well-meaning elder, often a teacher, has instilled in a child a lifelong abhorrence of verse by drooling over an unfathomable passage from Chaucer – or worse still, insisting that a pupil "explain" a poem, as if it were a riddle to which an answer should be provided.

(Simon Armitage, "Poetry Should be Subversive," *the Guardian*, June 12, 2012)

Inquisitive

1. A few years ago I wrote a book which dealt in part with the difficulties of the English in India. Feeling that they would have had no difficulties in India themselves, the Americans read the book freely. The more they read it the better it made them feel, and a cheque to the author was the result. I bought a wood with the cheque. It is not a large wood – it contains scarcely any trees, and it is intersected, blast it, by a public footpath. Still, it is the first property that I have owned, so it is right that other people should participate in my shame, and should ask themselves, in accents that will vary with horror, this very important question: What is the effect of property upon the character? Don't let's touch on economics; the effect of private ownership upon the community as a whole is another question – a more important question, perhaps, but another one. Let's keep to psychology. If you own things, what's their effect on you? What's the effect on me of my wood?

(E.M. Forster, "My Wood," *Abinger Harvest*, London: Edward Arnold (Publishers) Ltd., 1936, reprinted 1965, 33)

2. To govern is to choose how the revenue raised from taxes is spent. So far so good, or bad. But some people earn more money than others. Should they pay proportionately more money to the government than those who earn less? And if they do pay more money are they entitled to more

services than those who pay less or those who pay nothing at all? And should those who pay nothing at all because they have nothing get anything? These matters are of irritable concern to our rulers, and of some poignancy to the rest.

> (Gore Vidal, "Homage to Daniel Shays," *Selected Essays*, ed. Jay Parini, London: Abacus, 2007, 35)

3. It is a hundred years ago today since Forster died; we celebrate his centenary indeed within a few months of the bicentenary of Beethoven, within a few weeks of that of Blake. What special tribute shall we bring him? The question is not easy to answer, and were he himself still alive he would no doubt reply, "My work is my truest memorial." It is the reply that a great artist can always be trusted to make. Conscious of his lofty mission, endowed with the divine gift of self-expression, he may rest content. He is at peace, doubly at peace. But we, we who are not great artists, only the recipients of their bounty – what shall we say about Forster? What can we say that has not already been said about Beethoven, about Blake? Whatever shall we say? The Dean of Dulborough, preaching last Sunday in his own beautiful cathedral, struck perhaps the truest note.

> (E.M. Forster, "My Own Centenary, From The Times of AD2027," *Abinger Harvest*, London: Edward Arnold (Publishers) Ltd., 1936, reprinted 1965, 74-5)

4. A persistent strand of moralizing has stressed sincerity in prose composition. Don't put on airs. Write about what you have personally experienced. Try to develop a style of your own. The sum of such counsel is a text from Polonius. He ends his platitudinous admonitions to his son Laertes with the famous "To thine own self be true". What precedes this ringing phrase, unhappily, is more sensible advice on how to fabricate a safe and expedient self to be true to. Laertes, had he been a bit wittier, could have sensibly replied, "Self? – what self?" So a student might well reply to the preaching of such moralists "How can I be sincere when I haven't yet put together a self to be true to?"

> (Richard A. Lanham, *Style: An Anti-Textbook*, New Haven and London: Yale University Press, 1974, 115)

Examples of Various Combinations

1. Narrative / Inquisitive

Some time ago, while driving through a heavily forested region of northern Wisconsin, I came into a huge area that had been laid waste by logging in the nineteenth century. It was nearly a century later, yet all that remained inside this mighty forest were countless stumps. The image was vivid: nature was wounded and the wound would not heal. This image, and my reaction, still stick in my mind: here was nature cut down, held down, killed. Reflecting on it now, I find myself wondering in the face of such devastation, do we always invest nature with phantasies, say, of an injured mother? Do we always destroy, repair, thieve, live from Mother Nature? Do we need these phantasies, both to exploit nature and to moderate our incursions? Can we engage with an inanimate nature as plain pragmatists? Can we know nature without anthropomorphism and yet with respect?

> (Karl Figlio, "Knowing, loving and hating nature: a psychoanalytic view,"*Future Natural: Nature, Science, Culture*, ed. George Robertson, Melinda Mash, Lisa Tickner, Jon Bird, Barry Curtis and Tim Putman, Routledge, London and NY, 1996, 73)

2. Preparatory / Inquisitve

The Maures are my favourite mountains, a range of old rounded mammalian granite which rise (sic) three thousand feet above the coast of Provence. In summer they are covered by dark forests of cork and pine, with paler interludes on the northern slopes of bright splay-trunked chestnut and an undergrowth of arbutus and bracken. There is always water in the Maures, and the mountains are green throughout the summer, never baked like the limestone or like the Southern Alps a slagheap of gritty oyster-shell. They swim in the golden light in which the radiant ebony green of their vegetation stands out against the sky, a region hardly inhabited yet friendly as those dazzling landscapes of Claude and Poussin in which shepherds and sailors from antique ships meander under incongruous elms. Harmonies of light and colour, drip of water over fern; they inculcate in those who stay long in the Midi and whose brains are addled by iodine, a habit of moralizing, a brooding about causes. What makes men divide up into nations and go to war? Why do they live in cities? And what is the true relationship between Nature and Man?

> (Cyril Connolly, "The Ant-Lion," *The Condemned Playground Essays: 1927-1944*, London: Routledge, 1945, reprinted 1946, 231)

3. Corrective / Preparatory or Preparatory / Corrective

Going all the way back to Paul Samuelson's first edition in 1948, every economics textbook I know of has argued that the government should intervene in the market to discourage activities that damage the environment. The usual recommendation is to do so either by charging fees for the right to engage in such nasty activities – a.k.a. "pollution taxes'"– or by auctioning off rights to pollute. Indeed, as the extraordinary response to the climate-change statement reminds us, the idea of pollution taxes is one of those iconic positions, like free trade, that commands the assent of virtually every card-carrying economist. Yet while pollution and related "negative externalities" such as traffic congestion are obvious problems, in practice, efforts to make markets take environmental costs into account are few and far between. So economists who actually believe the things they teach generally support a much more aggressive program of environmental protection than the ones we actually have. True, they tend to oppose detailed regulations that tell people exactly how they must reduce pollution, preferring schemes that provide a financial incentive to pollute less but leave the details to the private sector. But I would be hard pressed to think of a single economist not actually employed by an anti-environmental lobbying operation who believes that the United States should protect the environment less, not more, than it currently does.

> (Paul Krugman, *The Accidental Theorist and Other Dispatches from the Dismal Science,* London: Penguin Books, 1999, 169)

The revision of conventional masculinity lies at the center of the corpus of William Faulkner. Throughout Faulkner's novels, characters whose compulsions to follow traditional but outdated attitudes of gender and whose role-playing, usually driven by historical and cultural prescription, distinguishes them as old-fashioned 'men,' inevitably occupy a prominent place in the narratives. Just as inevitably, these Faulknerian idealists are also doomed to failure or death, or both. Early critics of Faulkner typically treated these failures sympathetically. For them, the idealism of these characters seemed to represent some sense of retained honor, some admirable integrity in the face of worsening times. This honor and integrity may never have saved these Faulknerian males, but early critics generally used them to define the novels' idea – and ideal – of masculinity. More recent opinion, however, has quite rightly bucked this tendency.

> (David Rogers, "The Masculinity of Faded Blue:
> V.K. Ratliff and Faulkner's Creation of
> Transpositional Space," *The Faulkner Journal*, XV,
> 1&2, Fall 1999/Spring 2000, 125)

EXERCISE 7a: Adding Formal Introductory Paragraphs

1. Return to your argumentative draft and now add a formal introductory paragraph, choosing from one of the four most common types that you have imitated.

2. Repeat this step by substituting in turn each of the other three common types for your original choice. See which works best and why.

3. Repeat step 2 with a formal introductory paragraph that combines more than one main type.

Current Stages in Our Writing Process for Argumentative Essays

1. **The Procrastination Stage:** Incorporate whatever form of procrastination puts you in the right frame of mind to begin writing.

2. **The Freewriting Stage:** Set aside around 30 minutes and write with abandon about your topic. Then take a break.

3. **The Planning Stage:** Reread your freewriting and then organize the ideas, trying not to become too attached to your plan.

4. **The Mastermind Stage:** Compose a mastermind draft, writing or typing yourself to a conclusion.

5. **The Argumentative or Persuasive Stage:** Copy the conclusion at the end of your mastermind draft and paste it at the beginning.

6. **The Weighty Stage – Thesis Statements:** Revise your newly pasted conclusion into a more effective thesis.

7. **The Content Stage – Paragraphing:** Substantiate and refine the content of your essay and check your style.

8. **The Stylish Stage – Formal Introductory Paragraphs:** Consider which of the four most common types of formal introductory paragraphs (or combination of types) may be most appropriate for your essay and topic. Once you have chosen, insert the formal introductory paragraph before your thesis statement. (If you have used a mapping paragraph in your earlier draft then you should remove it and replace it with your new formal introductory paragraph.) Your thesis will then appear at the bottom of your formal introductory paragraph or at or near the top of your second paragraph. (Your choice may differ for different essays.) The objective, as you know, is to ease your readers into your argument in a way that will engage them and enhance your chances of persuading them of your thesis.

CHAPTER 5

The Submission Stage: Punctuation Made Easy

Always leave yourself enough time to reread the last drafts of your essays before you submit them. If necessary, use spell-check to ensure that you have spelled all of your words correctly and been consistent with your American or British usage. Also double check your punctuation and take a final look at your thesis. And, when you do, I will ask you to follow this basic advice for now: *do not use any form of punctuation other than a period (or full stop) without knowing why you are using it.* If you are not wholly sure of the official grammatical reason for using other forms of punctuation, in other words, then do not use them. It is almost always better to trust the quality and correctness of your syntax to express your meanings and avoid all punctuation with the exception of the period than it is arbitrarily to include a range of punctuation just because you think its inclusion will make your writing appear more sophisticated.

This advice may seem overly simplistic. But even the least experienced writers compose reasonably sound and syntactically correct sentences. More to the point, very few ever use periods or question marks incorrectly between complete sentences. Thus, only rarely do I encounter inadvertent sentence fragments such as this one: "He never comes to the seminars. Because he hates waking up early in the morning." Rarely do developing writers make a mistake like this one: "All students should note the change to the new procedure for library loans they should remember to use this new procedure from the start of the semester."

Yet it's the rare novice writer who consistently knows when or how to use commas, colons, or semicolons correctly. As a consequence, most errors of punctuation arise when they misuse these forms of punctuation. Indeed, untrained writers usually seem to insert them almost haphazardly, as if when it seems opportune or when they've not used any of them in a long time. It's as if they think they must include a range of punctuation if they want their writing to be taken seriously. Yet, almost without fail, such a strategy of random guesswork causes more confusion than it solves. Both writer and reader are usually better off if the writer sticks to what she knows – if she resists the temptation to take a chance with her punctuation.

So let me repeat. It is prudent never to use any punctuation except a period (or question mark) unless you are one hundred percent positive that you know that you are using other forms of punctuation correctly (not *think* you are using them correctly but *know* you are). If you follow this simple rule, you will eliminate the overwhelming majority of your mistakes of punctuation at a stroke. And you will not appear a simpleton. Nor will you often confuse or distort the meanings of your sentences. For there are only a very few times when the form of punctuation you use directly determines the meaning of your sentence. In the vast majority of cases writing grammatically correct sentences will convey your meaning accurately and clearly.

Don't take any of what I say to mean that I want to discourage you from learning to punctuate correctly, however. Learning punctuation correctly is certainly worth the effort. When placed appropriately, punctuation can add emphasis, pace, and clarity to even the most polished sentences, and you may have noticed that I punctuate fairly liberally, as do the writers of many of the examples of good practice in this book. But, then, I have been trained over more years than I care to think about. So learn the rules that govern the use of these other types of punctuation before you include them in your essays. But until then stick to the good old period along with the occasional question mark and exclamation point. Your essays will contain many fewer mistakes. And they will be just as easy to read.

Common Types of Punctuation

Period

Periods or full stops signal the end of a fully realized thought expressed in a sentence that contains its own subject and its own main verb or predicate. Given this working definition, you may put a period at the end of every such complete sentence that you write that does not ask a question. For it is always correct to put a period between two complete sentences no matter how simple or complex each may be.

Examples of Periods Used Correctly

1. I did not know you were so strict. I would have been willing to stop earlier.

2. Never use any form of punctuation that you do not know for certain how to use. The consequences for trying to appear sophisticated are much worse than the consequences of being simple and correct.

3. Honor the period. It has served great writers well and it will continue to serve great writers well long into the future. Commas, semicolons, and colons are worthy fellow travelers for the experienced writer. But writers still struggling to master the nuances of good thesis statements and formal introductory paragraphs and still learning how to generate their ideas across well-developed paragraphs are well advised to put their trust in the period and leave the other forms of punctuation aside for the time being. *(Most writers would place a comma after "well" in line one and some would after "writers" in line four and after "paragraphs" in line seven. A few might even use a comma between "paragraphs" and "and" or even between "period" and "and." But the final sentence is grammatically correct as it is.)*

4. Look closely at a few sentences of your favorite writer. Copy those sentences taking out all forms of punctuation except the period. See if the sentences still make sense to you. They should. Then ask yourself why the writer has used the other forms of punctuation. Answering these questions will help you to begin to understand the rules for using the other forms of punctuation.

5. When you revise your essays always ask yourself why you have used different forms of punctuation when you have. Explain to yourself in each case the rule governing your use. If you cannot provide one or you cannot find one in a reference book somewhere then you probably want to eliminate that punctuation and if it has come between two

complete sentences replace it with a period. *(Inserting a comma after "your essays" in the first sentence would be correct. So too would placing one after "somewhere" in the third. Convention probably dictates the insertion of a comma after "punctuation" and before "and" in the last compound, complex sentence as well as after "and" and after "sentences." But not inserting commas in these instances would not be wrong and your sentences would still make sense.)*

Comma

Commas generally cause more problems for would-be essayists than any other type of punctuation. Some of these problems occur because these writers don't know that in almost all cases we use commas in pairs when we insert them internally within our sentences. This minor problem, however, amounts to little more than an irritation to most readers. Most readers or lecturers will tolerate it, although you can avoid having to depend on their tolerance if you resist the temptation to insert a comma or commas willy-nilly into your sentences without knowing precisely why you have done so.

The most serious misuse of commas, however, is not so innocent or tolerable. It occurs when writers substitute a comma for a period between complete sentences. It is never correct to include a comma in this way. Doing so creates what is known as a comma splice, and most teachers of writing will be less likely to excuse this error. It is so easy to avoid it, however, that you should really never make it. Just rely on a period instead.

Examples of Comma Splice

1. Jazz is my favorite music, pizza is my favorite food. *(Jazz is my favorite music. Pizza is my favorite food.)*
2. Whenever I see red I feel faint, I don't know why. *(Whenever I see red, I feel faint. I don't know why.)*
3. The events of the last few weeks have left the world in shock, it will take a long time for all of us to recover. *(The events of the last few weeks have left the world in shock. It will take a long time for all of us to recover.)*
4. In some climates love is liked for its own sake, it is the only

cause of happiness, it is life itself. (*In some climates, love is liked for its own sake. It is the only cause of happiness. It is life itself.*)

5. You must have a valid ticket before entering the train, otherwise you will be subject to a fine of at least ten pounds. (*actual notice at one English station*) (**You must have a valid ticket before entering the train. Otherwise you will be subject to a fine of at least ten pounds.**)

As you can see, you can readily avoid this problem by using a period instead of the comma between what are complete sentences. There are, however, just a few instances when the use of a comma affects the meaning of a well-constructed sentence, and here they are.

When to Use a Comma

In spite of my cautions about the potential dangers of using commas when you are not absolutely sure of your reasons, there are some instances when you will want to insert commas in order to ensure that the meaning of your sentences is clear.

1. To accompany a coordinating conjunction in the creation of a compound sentence (when using a USA style guide)

   a. Knowing the rules of punctuation is important for all writers, *and* most series ones do know them even if they choose to ignore them at times for various effects. (*The two complete sentences are joined by the coordinating conjunction "and."*)

   b. Transitional devices can take a variety of forms, *but* the most common ones convey some relationship of time or place or sequence. (*The two complete sentences are joined by the coordinating conjunction "but."*)

   c. Students should continue to imitate good practice, *for* only imitation can really allow them to experience different styles first hand. (*The two complete sentences are joined by the coordinating conjunction "for."*)

    d. Fourteen students signed up for the essay writing course when it was first announced, *yet* forty-four showed up at seminar room on the first day of classes. *(The two complete sentences are joined by the coordinating conjunction "yet.")*

2. To separate a list or a series of similar parts of speech or construction (a comma before the final item is optional)

    a. Such a series may include objects, people, abstract ideas, or even parts of sentences.

    b. Bill, Jane, Fred, Sally, and Sue won the four hundred meters relay, the fifteen hundred meters relay, and the five thousand meters relay at our school Olympics.

    c. People believe that only the famous, the busy, and the talented have the power to solicit funds from the rich, notice from the press, and envy from the opposition.

    d. Max Bohr stood virtually still, had a horrible mumble, was often inarticulate and inaudible, and would often repeat a single word endlessly when engrossed in his thought.

3. To indicate whether clarifying information is inessential or presumed known by the reader or listener. (The use of a comma implies that you think the reader knows beforehand the information that you are emphasizing. The absence of commas implies that the reader does not already know the information that you are reiterating.)

    a. Bill Clinton's wife, Hillary, has her own career as a lawyer and politician. *(The presence of the comma indicates that I believe readers will know that Bill Clinton's wife is named Hillary.)*

    b. When the mob came for the mayor of the town, Hari, his son fled into a nearby patch of overgrown wasteland. *(The presence of the comma suggests most readers would know that Hari is the mayor.)*

c. On 11 February 1990, Nelson Mandela came through the gates of Victor Verster prison hand in hand with his wife, Winnie, towards a crowd of supporters and a mob of the world media. *(Here again the comma implies that the writer believes readers will know that Nelson Mandela's second wife was named Winnie.)*

d. My dog Spot is a good dog. *(The absence of commas implies that I do not think that my reader already knows that my dog is named Spot. In this case, including the name is essential information in the sentence, and so therefore I do not place commas around "Spot.")*

4. To set off internal connectives

a. In the case of the plastic arts, *for example,* the native artist who wishes at whatever cost to create a national work of art shuts himself up in a stereotypical reproduction of details.

b. It is, *indeed,* only at a certain stage in the development of the realistic intelligence of a people that a tragic faith can emerge.

c. It is worthwhile, *however,* to examine carefully the consequences of accepting the notion that writing styles are distinguished by deviations from some abstract norm.

d. The past, *therefore,* has been far deeper and more pregnant with novelty than any short-term realist can envisage.

5. To set off internal qualifiers or asides

a. Here, *it seems to me,* is the reading of the riddle that puzzles so many of us.

b. Abraham Lincoln, *we have said,* revealed his greatness only after he reached the highest office.

c. Good reading and good writing are, *first and last,* lots of work.

d. The only justification for military action, *they argued,* would arise if the government stopped all of the traffic through the canal.

6. To set off internal dependent clauses

    a. While Henry, *as his friends never tired of pointing out,* had always been able to rely on a private income, Fred had left school at the age of twelve to help with his family's small business.

    b. I took the long way around on the subway and, *because I was heading for downtown,* the city seemed to have all of the charm of a Utrillo painting.

    c. Spike marks on the surface of a green, *if they occur in crucial areas,* are bound to affect the roll of the putts.

    d. But then, *if I am right,* certain professions of education must be wrong when they say that they can put knowledge into the soul which was not there before, like sight into blind eyes.

7. To follow an introductory clause or phrase that is long enough to potentially entangle readers in a complicated sentence structure

    a. *If the sun were to disappear suddenly,* the earth would be instantly thrown out of its orbit and would freeze in deep space. *(The opening is a dependent clause because it contains a complete sentence beginning with a subordinate conjunction, in this case "If.")*

    b. *Despite all of the fashionable blather about individual voices,* most poets use and reuse the common parlance of the age with only a slight personal accent. *(Here, the opening is only a phrase since it lacks a main verb of its own and so it does not express a complete thought.)*

    c. *One of the most ubiquitous and widely advertised commodities of the late nineteenth century,* the cigarette occupies a prominent and honorable position in the work of Oscar Wilde. *(The opening here serves as an apostrophe, which is a word or phrase that redefines the word or words that follows or precedes it, in this case "cigarette.")*

d. *Dwarfed by the scale of their undertaking,* the weary men inched their way through the ice and snow on the mountains. *(The opening phrase modifies or describes "the weary men.")*

e. *If the writing of an outline prior to the writing of an essay assures superior organization,* it would seem to follow that the student essay that had been preceded by an outline would rank higher by teacher evaluation than essays that had not. Yet studies, conducted over years by a range of academics, have revealed no correlation between the presence of an outline and the grade students received. *(The phrase beginning "conducted" modifies or describes "studies.")*

There are two other common types of punctuation that I suggest you resist unless and until you know the rules of punctuation very well. These are the semicolon and the colon.

Semicolon

Some writers claim to be in love with the semicolon, but, for me, semicolons should serve practically as the persona non grata of punctuation. They are correct in only two instances. Both occur rarely, and in only one instance are semicolons essential to convey meaning appropriately. The first appears between two consecutive complete sentences, the thoughts or ideas of which you believe relate to each other significantly more closely than the thoughts or ideas in the rest of your sentences, or at least the majority of them. In such instances, a semicolon signals this particularly close link between the ideas or thoughts of these sentences. But you do not have to use a semicolon between such sentences. A period is just as acceptable and correct, and the ideas in your sentences will remain just as close. By contrast, if you substitute semicolons too often on such occasions, you will contradict the reasoning behind their substitution. In other words, if you link too many of your sentences with semicolons, then your semicolons will cease to indicate any more special connection than those separated by periods. So, here again it's probably best to play it safe. Dispense with the semicolon until you have gained more experience. Rely instead on the period. You'll generally be correct when you do.

The second correct use of the semicolon occurs when you have a series of items, one or some or all of which contain commas within them. I doubt that you'll depend on this construction very often, but, when you do, you will see immediately why the semicolon serves you best. The semicolon will allow your reader to distinguish the items in your series from the internal characteristics of individual items. Therefore I have provided examples below to guide you. But when was the last time you listed such complicated items in a series in one of your essays?

Examples of the Correct Use of the Semicolon

1. Semicolons used between two complete sentences that the writer apparently assumes are more closely related than most of the rest of the sentences

    a. It seemed ridiculous to stop a man playing high-class cricket rather than watching rain fall in London; yet if Daniel were to be allowed leeway others would expect it as well.

    b. I went into the garden; there were flowers everywhere.

    c. Philosophers may deride subjective notions of communication with some justification; as analytical tools they are overly flawed.

    d. The fate of the murderous general became a matter of fierce debate among the coup leaders. Some wanted his execution; others favored exile.

    e. In connected writing, the topic sentence varies greatly in how explicit it is in designating the thesis of the paragraph. Sometimes it is quite explicit; sometimes it is a mere sign pointing to the turn the new paragraph is going to take.

2. Semicolons used between items in a series when one or more of those items contain a comma

    a. The circus included clowns, some of whom wore red tuxedos and long pointed shoes; animal acts involving big cats, prancing horses, and small monkeys; and a couple who did cartwheels on a

174

high wire without a net below. *(The series includes "clowns," "acts," and "couple.")*

b. In selecting a co-captain we should consider the candidate's ability to captain the side, for whatever reason, in the short term; his ability to advise and help the captain; and his potential for captaincy and learning. *(The series includes "ability to captain," "ability to advise," and "potential for captaincy.")*

c. Neither the uneducated nor the uninformed of the truth will make good government officials because they will have no single aim of duty that will rule their actions, private as well as public; never act upon compulsion, always assuming that they are already living apart in the islands of the blest; too often be open to bribes. *(The series includes "no single aim," "never act," and "be open.")*

d. For us, then, the term *essay* will always signify an argumentative essay, an essay that attempts to persuade readers of a single main idea; to change (or open) the minds of our readers; and to convince them that the thesis or central argument of our essay is valid and well-considered. *(The series includes "to persuade," "to change," and "to convince.")*

e. As Bacon illustrates, no good essayist convinces a skeptical audience simply by shouting at them, so to speak, and, in many successful argumentative essays, the writer, following Bacon's example, may well indicate where apparently opposing ideas are valid, or might be; show an understanding and respect for those ideas; or at least explain why their validity remains an issue. *(This series includes "indicate," "show," and "explain.")*

Colon

Few novice writers rely very much on colons. Yet, paradoxically, colons represent the only valid exception to my period-or-full-stops-only policy, although here again one key rule can also govern our use of them: rely on a colon (or dash) only before a sentence-ending explanation, a sentence-ending quotation, or the introduction of direct speech at the end of a sentence. Even in these cases, a period will also be correct as long as the explanation that follows your complete sentence is itself a complete sentence. Only when the explanation does not form a complete sentence *must* you employ a colon, as you can see in the examples below.

Examples of Colons When a Period Would Also Be Correct

1. He attempted to portray the central idea behind his art: truth can only be felt. It cannot be spoken. *(He attempted to portray the central idea behind his art. Truth can only be felt. It cannot be spoken.)*

2. The use of letters was not known in the north of Europe till long after the institution of bards: the records of families of their patrons, their own, and more ancient poems were handed down by tradition. *(The use of letters was not known in the north of Europe till long after the institution of bards. The records of families of their patrons, their own, and more ancient poems were handed down by tradition.)*

3. Graphology may be only a pseudoscience, but it rests on a genuine insight: there is some essential connection between handwriting and character. *(Graphology may be only a pseudoscience, but it rests on a genuine insight. There is some essential connection between handwriting and character.)*

4. Part of the reason a city needs a certain critical mass of enterprise and opportunity to create a self-sustaining culture is economic: artists need employment. *(Part of the reason a city needs a certain critical mass of enterprise and opportunity to create a self-sustaining culture is economic. Artists need employment.)*

5. My basic point is very simple indeed: you cannot underestimate the capacity for invention that any individual in need possesses. *(My basic point is very simple indeed. You cannot underestimate the capacity for invention that any individual in need possesses.)*

Examples of Colons When a Period Would NOT Be Correct

1. The fall of the Berlin Wall provided a new arena for the International Monetary Fund: managing the transition to a market economy in the former Soviet Union and the Communist bloc countries in Europe. *(The part of the sentence following the colon is not a complete sentence in and of itself.)*

2. To focus on the dramatic is to look in writing for some active consent to a chastening fact: the fact that words exist independently of the uses to which anyone wants to put them. *(The part of the sentence following the colon does not contain a primary verb.)*

3. The novel *The Picture of Dorian Gray* catalogues the forms of identification of the ideal consumer as dandy: a receptacle and bearer of sensations, poser and posed, with a consistent identity, no moral self. *(The part of the sentence following the colon lacks a primary verb and so is not a complete sentence.)*

4. Everyone recognizes the right of revolution: that is, the right to refuse allegiance to and to resist the government when its tyranny or its inefficiency is great and unendurable. *(The part of the sentence following the colon is not a complete sentence in and of itself. The word "is" serves as the verb for clause beginning with "when.")*

5. My experience tells me that players go to coaches in the same frame of mind that patients go to doctors: as if they are sick and want to be cured. *(The part of the sentence following the colon is a dependent clause and not a complete sentence.)*

Examples of Colons Before Sentence-Ending Quotations

Colons before sentence-ending quotations are only correct when those quotations follow a complete sentence and, in effect, explain it. When the quotation completes the sentence, that is, when it forms part of the syntax of the sentence, then it is incorrect to use the colon. Using a comma or semicolon before a sentence-ending quotation that follows a complete sentence is always incorrect.

1. The attitude from the boys in the backroom could not have been more dismissive: "You go on about your business."

2. The biographer described handwriting's special ability to communicate the inner state of its author: "Script's primary power is to convey the cursive flow of human thought, from brain to hand to pen to ink to eye."

3. "What is the secret of life?" the poet once asked a famous painter. "With anyone else," the poet said, "the answer would have begun with an ironic laugh, but the famous painter answered the question in straightforward, pragmatic terms: "The secret of life," he said, "is to have a task, something you devote your entire life to, something you bring everything to, every minute." *(Note the quotation marks around the quoted explanation. They are there in this case because the explanation itself contains a quote from the painter.)*

4. One newspaper, in an editorial in 1980, called attention to the Corps of Engineers' efforts to prevent the great shift at Old River, and concluded with this sentiment: "Who will win as this slow-motion confrontation between humankind and nature goes on? No one really knows."

5. In the historian's words, "the modern foreign policy of Great Britain has been primarily a struggle for profitable markets of investment," and what applied to Great Britain was equally true of France and Germany. But a second historian put it a few years later in a sharper way: "Working men may proceed to slay each other in order to decide whether it shall be French or German financiers who shall export the surplus capital."

Apostrophes

The apostrophe does not really fit into the same category of punctuation as a period, question mark, comma, semicolon, or colon. I mention it here only because there's really no excuse for misusing the apostrophe, even if inexperienced writers often seem to have great difficulty remembering the rule for its use. Yet there are generally only two instances when you require an apostrophe. One is to create possessives. The other is to form contractions (single words combining two words with the loss of one or more letters). To test whether you are creating a possessive, you need to ask yourself this question: can I place my possessive directly before the word to which it refers, insert the word *of* between them, and still have my sentence make the same sense? Here is an example: "Mary's sister lives next door to me." Can we change the sentence to read "The sister of Mary lives next door to me?" The answer is clearly yes, so an apostrophe is required. When the answer to any similar change of order is "No," however, then you should not add an apostrophe. The word you need is probably a plural, not a possessive.

In this example above, we know that we have applied our apostrophe correctly. If, by contrast, you use the apostrophe as did the hot dog seller I saw outside the front gate of the New York Giants' football stadium last season, then you will know that you have inserted it incorrectly. "Hot dog's for sale" read his sign. But plainly there is nothing that this "dog" possesses. (We can't say "the hot of dog for sale," can we?) Instead the seller had wanted to indicate that he had more than one hot dog to sell. He had had many hot dogs he wanted to shift. But, to communicate that idea correctly, he needed instead the simple plural form (hot dogs) not the possessive. I, on the other hand, have put in the apostrophe correctly when referring to the New York Giants' football stadium, for my use passes the rearrangement test. I can rephrase the sentence and say with full confidence "I saw the hot dog salesman outside the football stadium of the New York Giants."

Examples of Possessives Used Correctly

1. The *nation's place* in the world seems continually open to debate among both the politicians and the general population. *(the place of the nation)*

2. Despite the eruption of military coups, civil strife, and political instability, a sense of optimism about *Africa's future* prevailed throughout the 1960s. *(the future of Africa)*

3. *Humankind's whole history* is one of transcendence and of self-examination that has led to angelic heights of sacrifice as well as bleak regions of despair. *(the whole history of humankind)*

4. Practically everyone has heard of *Einstein's theory of relativity*, but hardly anyone knows what it means in practical terms. *(the theory of relativity of Einstein)*

5. Over the past generation we have, according to lots of

commentators and social and political scientists, seen a marked decline in *workers' rights. (the rights of workers – the apostrophe goes after the 's' when the possessive is plural)*

The second case when you might use an apostrophe occurs when you create a contraction. A contraction is one word formed through the combination of two words with an apostrophe replacing the letter or letters you omit. For example, combining *will* and *not* to form *won't* or *can* and *not* to form *can't* creates contractions. The same is true when you form the word *we're* from we and *are*. Most writers handle these types of contractions easily enough. The one exception involves the word *it's* which is formed by combining *it* and *is*. Many people confuse this contraction with the possessive *its*. As we have seen above, most possessives require the apostrophe. But the possessive *its* does not. So, when you are editing your essays, always test your use of *its* and *it's*. If you can substitute *it is*, then you need to use *it's*. If you can apply our conversion step above, then use *its*. In any case, always ask your editor or lecturer if she minds whether you include contractions in your essays. Some may object. But others won't (will not).

Examples of Possessives and Apostrophes Used Correctly

1. The government does not usually consider it's (*it is*) any of its (*possessive*) business to interfere in the affairs of so-called free trade.

2. It's (*It is*) almost always one of the big four teams that wins the Super Bowl.

3. Some people apparently still think it's (*it is*) natural for women to spend twice as much time doing housework than their husbands.

4. Doing math remains a mystery for some people throughout their whole lives, but its (*possessive – the difficulty of doing math*) difficulty is an even greater mystery.

5. Doing math remains a mystery for some people throughout their whole lives, but it's (*it is – contraction*) impossible for others to fathom why.

EXERCISE 8
Editing your Drafts:
Punctuation and Submission

1. Spell-check your argumentative draft.

2. Reread that draft as an editor might. Check each comma, semicolon, and/or colon, and ask yourself if you are certain why you have used each one. Whenever you are unsure, eliminate that form of punctuation. Stick instead to periods, and, if necessary, revise your sentence constructions so that they are clear enough to make sense without any other punctuation.

3. Check all instances when you have used an apostrophe in an attempt to indicate possession or you have used a contraction. Test to see if you have used the apostrophe correctly and change where necessary.

4. Ask yourself if your current argumentative draft is now ready for submission as a final essay.

Overall Stages in Our Writing Process for Argumentative Essays

1. **The Procrastination Stage:** Incorporate whatever form of procrastination puts you in the right frame of mind to begin writing.

2. **The Freewriting Stage:** Set aside around 30 minutes and write with abandon about your topic. Then take a break.

3. **The Planning Stage:** Reread your freewriting and then organize the ideas, trying not to become too attached to your plan.

4. **The Mastermind Stage:** Compose a mastermind draft, writing or typing yourself to a conclusion.

5. **The Argumentative or Persuasive Stage:** Copy the conclusion at the end of your mastermind draft and paste it at the beginning.

6. **The Weighty Stage – Thesis Statements:** Revise your newly pasted conclusion into a more effective thesis.

7. **The Content Stage – Paragraphing:** Substantiate and refine the content of your essay and check your style.

8. **The Stylish Stage – Formal Introductory Paragraphs**: Insert one of the four most common types of formal introductory paragraphs (or combination of types) before your thesis statement.

9. **The Refinement Stage:** Reread your essay again to ensure you have expressed yourself as clearly and coherently as you can. Then read your thesis one more time to see if you can make it even more precise, declarative, and succinct. Check your spelling and punctuation carefully and make sure that you have used the right conventions and the correct system of referencing as per the instructions of your intended publication or lecturer.

CONCLUSION

Congratulations! You've now completed all of the steps in a single process that will help you write good argumentative essays, and you've had a chance to practice each step through exercises and imitation of examples from experienced writers. I hope that by now you have begun to understand our few rhetorical principles for writing good essays and, more importantly, begun to be able to apply them. But, if not, don't worry. As I've said throughout, and Stevenson warned us at the very beginning of the book, as aspiring writers we must expect to fall short at first as we struggle with old habits and attempt to acquire new styles. The key is persistence. You must practice, practice, practice.

Essay writing, as I have said, draws on what speakers and writers, including you, do and have done naturally for centuries. If you pay attention to the ways people speak and work hard to emulate the natural structures that rhetoricians have classified for us and that good writers demonstrate time and time again, then you can create these structures as well. Moreover, if you are willing to accept that writing essays involves a process of redrafting and revision and your assumption of the complementary roles of reader and writer, then you will be able to write argumentative essays that are more coherent and more persuasive. More importantly, you will, I hope, gain a sense of satisfaction from discovering more of what you think and expressing those thoughts more clearly. For these reasons, I encourage you to return to the exercises and examples in the book as you continue to improve your essay-writing skills. Students, particularly, can forget some of what they have learned during periods away from university. Practice may not always lead to perfection, but it does always make the average better. For now, however, please look at the maxims that follow. And see how well you can do on the quiz on the final page.

Maxims to Remember

1. Argumentative essays should not be the products of abstract thinking alone.
2. Writing successful argumentative essays involves a process of key stages.
3. Good writing is a learned craft requiring a range of techniques.
4. Good writing is good rewriting.
5. Writing well requires you to read attentively.
6. Essays develop best from the general to the specific, the specific to the general, or the least important to the most important.
7. Using explicit transitional devices to link sentences and thoughts wherever appropriate will help to ensure that your essays are coherent.
8. It is almost always better to use "this" as a demonstrative adjective followed by a clarifying word or phrase than it is to use it as a demonstrative pronoun.
9. Resist inserting commas or semicolons unless and until you are certain you know the rules for their usage.
10. Practice, practice, practice.

Review Quiz to Demonstrate Your Understanding

1. Explain the difference between the concept of writing as a process and writing as product of your ideas.
2. What is the object of the freewriting stage of our writing process? What is the best attitude to take during this stage of your process?
3. What mainly distinguishes mapping paragraphs?
4. How does the mastermind stage of your writing process relate to the planning stage? Why should you be cautious about relying too strictly on any form of planning?
5. How do you transform a mastermind draft into your first argumentative essay draft?

6. What is a thesis and what qualities distinguish a good thesis?

7. What distinguishes a generative model paragraph from a topic sentence paragraph?

8. Write two examples of each type of paragraph. Make sure each consists of no fewer than seven sentences.

9. List five or more types of transitional devices. Explain which device is your favorite and why. Write two examples of each of the types of transitional devices you have identified above.

10. What are the four most common categories of formal introductory paragraphs?

11. Write an example of each of these four categories of formal introductory paragraphs.

12. Paraphrase our golden rule about punctuation. Then write two sentences in which you use a colon correctly and two in which you use commas correctly.

Simple Conventions for Writing Argumentative Essays

1. Some Conventions of General Presentation

Conventions may vary, and the ones below represent only a sample of good practice. So always use the ones required by your lecturer or editor or the publication to which you are submitting your essay. Get into the habit of consulting available handbooks and websites on style for more exact and comprehensive guidance.

a. Provide a title for your essays either on a separate title page or at the top of the first page of your essay. Ideally your title should suggest or imply the thesis of your essay in some way.

b. Double space your essays and use an acceptable font such as 12-point Times New Roman.

c. Indent each new paragraph five spaces from the left margin or, if your lecturer prefers, block off each new paragraph.

2. Conventions for Including Quotations in your Essays

a. Incorporate quotations shorter than three full lines into the text of your essay and correctly into your own sentences. Ensure that quotations fit grammatically and syntactically into your own sentences.

Examples

i. In the historian's words, "the modern foreign policy of Great Britain has been primarily a struggle for profitable markets of investment." A second historian put it a few years later in a sharper way when he observed that this foreign policy relied on an ironic exploitation of both sets of soldiers. For, he noted, it was based on the need of "[w]orking men to proceed to slay each other in order to decide whether it shall be French or German financiers who shall export the surplus capital." (*Note the brackets around the "w" of "workers in line 5. They indicate that the use of the quotation in the writer's sentence required a change from the original use of "Workers" with a capital "W."*)

ii. The biographer has described handwriting's special ability to communicate the inner state of its author. "Script's primary power," he said in an attempt to persuade his audience of handwriting's special ability to communicate the inner state of its writer, "is to convey the cursive flow of human thought, from brain to hand to pen to ink to eye – every waver, every loop, every character trembling with expression." He then paused for dramatic effect and looked around the crowded room. "Type," he said, "has no comparable warmth."

iii. "What is the secret of life?" a poet once asked a famous old painter. "With anyone else," the poet said, "the answer would have begun with an ironic laugh," but the painter answered the question in straightforward, pragmatic terms. "The secret of life," he said, "is to have a task, something you devote your entire life to, something you bring everything to, every minute of the day for the whole of your life."

Then he winked. "And the most important thing is," he said, "it must be something you cannot possibly do!" *(Note the way in which the added action – "Then he winked" and "he said" break up the previous longer version of the quotation and so requires commas and no centering of the quotation.)*

b. Indent and center on the page any quotation that is longer than three full lines of your text. Usually centering your longer quotations means indenting them ten spaces from the left and leaving approximately the same number of spaces from the right.

Examples

i. The situation was to her liking, and she freely gave interviews in which she discussed the candidacy of her husband. This trait of hers was the subject of a barbed paragraph in a popular magazine:

> The rumor that the ex-president, formerly recognized as the hero of the Right, will campaign around the country for both rival candidates is said to be false. His aides have vigorously denied that the report is true.

(Here that the writer precedes the quotation with a colon. He does so because the quotation follows and explains a complete sentence.)

ii. In his introduction to his book on the history of American intellectualism, the academic noted that

> the whole conceptual framework on which this type of work rested had worn away… Simultaneously, in a range of disciplines two working assumptions…have come under withering attack: firstly, the idea that cultures tend to be integrated, and secondly, that a shared culture supports and continues that integration…

(The writer here uses no punctuation before the quotation because the clause beginning "the entire" and ending with "crumbled away" completes the syntax of the sentence starting, "In his introduction."

The sentences in the quotation that follow therefore
are punctuated with periods. Notice the polyptotons
– "integrated" and "integration.")

3. Conventions for Reference Notations

a. Always note all references that have influenced you in your essay, including those that you do not quote specifically. If in doubt, always provide the reference. You do not want to risk being accused of plagiarism. Remember that in almost all cases, if not all, showing your references is a good thing because doing so demonstrates to your readers just how much research you have done to prepare for the essay. Depending on the instructions from your lecturers or editors, you should document your references either through footnotes or endnotes.

b. Footnotes appear at the end of the page on which the reference occurs or as near as possible.

c. Endnotes appear together at the end of your essays regardless of where exactly the individual reference appears. *The title "Endnotes" or "Notes" should appear on the page approximately six lines from the top. You should double-space your entries, indenting each citation five spaces from the left margin but not indenting subsequent lines. A superscripted citation number goes at the beginning of each citation, with one space after the number. Entries appear in the same numerical order as they appear in the text of your paper. Example: Tredinnick, Mark, Writing Well: The Essential Guide, Cambridge, Cambridge University Press, 2008, 7.*

4. Conventions for Bibliographies

a. Make sure that you adhere to the instructions of your editors or lecturers with respect to the specific system of conventions that you should use for your essay.

b. Place titles in alphabetical order according to author.

c. Underline or italicize titles of books and long poems. Elbow, Peter, *Writing with Power: Techniques for Mastering the Writing Process*, New York and Oxford: Oxford University Press, 1981, 1988 (book); Stanford, Frank, *The Battlefield Where the Moon Says I Love You*, Fayetteville, AR:

Lost Roads Publishers, 1984 (long poem).

d. Place quotation marks around the titles of short stories, essays, magazine, newspaper and encyclopedia articles, URLs, and poems that are not long enough to require italics: Updike, John, "The Pro," *Golf's Best Short Stories*, ed. Paul D. Staudohar, London: Souvenir Press, 2007, 25-30 (short story); Kael, Pauline, "Movies on Television," *The Oxford Book of Essays*, ed. John Gross, Oxford and New York: Oxford University Press, 1998, 595-606 (essay); Sorrell, Katherine, "Sense of Occasion," *Homes & Gardens*, December, 2010, 92-97 (magazine article); Brearley, Mike, "Captains Courageous Wage War of Wits," *the Guardian*, 2004 (newspaper article); Anonymous, "classical economics," *The Hutchinson Paperback Encyclopedia*, 1990. (encyclopedia article/entry); "Mind Map," *Wikipedia*, http://en.wikipedia.org/wiki/Mind_map (URL); Yeh, Jane, "On Ninjas," *The Ninjas*, Manchester: Carcanet, 2012, 23 (short poem in a collection of poems).

Common Rhetorical Topoi

An essay may need a clear thesis statement to structure its argument, but any good thesis statement must be followed by paragraphs that develop, support, and explain the main argument of the essay. The Introduction contains a diagram of our conventional structure for those paragraphs that make up the body of the essay. Chapter 3 explains ways in which you can generate supporting ideas as you write your individual paragraphs and ways in which you can make those individual paragraphs coherent, both internally and across each other. And, throughout, I have pointed out three common ways to organize your essays: from the least important to the most important; the general to the specific; or, in a few cases, the specific to the general. Although there are others, these strategies will generally serve you well in most instances.

Very occasionally, however, as you refine your paragraphs through your process of revision, you may think that you don't immediately seem to have enough ideas and you can't seem to generate more using the strategies I have set out. You may not see a clear progression of your argument along any of the three lines I have provided. In such instances, you may want to turn to more classical rhetorical devices. Such devices can provide additional pointers to help you. The first of these pointers has to do with what rhetoricians call "modes of appeal," of which generally there are three.

1. The appeal to reason.
2. The appeal to emotions.
3. The appeal to character.

The main rhetorical aids to invention, however, are formally referred to as topoi. I recommend that you consult Corbett for a complete explanation of topoi, but, for now, I will list the key ones for you, although there is no need to worry about which specific topoi or combination you may be using with each essay that you write. (See the advice by Harris and McDougall in the endnote related to them.)

Common Topoi

1. Definition

2. Comparison
a. Similarity
b. Difference
c. Degree

3. Relationships
a. Cause and Effect
b. Contraries
c. Contradiction
d. Antecedents
   and Consequences

4. Circumstances
a. Possible and
   Impossible
b. Past Fact and
   Fact

5. Testimony
a. Authority
b. Testimonial
c. Statistics

Notes

1 Richard Marius, *A Writer's Companion*, 3rd ed., New York: McGraw-Hill, Inc., 1991, 37.

2 Collete Dalute, "Do Writers Talk to Themselves?," *The Acquisition of Written Language: Response and Revision*, ed. Sarah Warshauer Freedman, Norwood, N.J: Ablex Publishing Corp, 1985, 133.

3 Edward P.J. Corbett, *Classical Rhetoric for the Modern Student*, 2nd ed., New York: Oxford University Press, 1971, 3.

4 Robert Louis Stevenson, "A College Magazine," *Memories and Portraits*, Cited in David Daiches, *Robert Louis Stevenson and his World*, London: Thames and Hudson, 1973, 28.

5 Colette Dalute, "Do Writers Talk to Themselves?," *The Acquisition of Written Language: Response and Revision*, ed. Sarah Warshauer Freedman, Norwood, N.J: Ablex Publishing Corp, 1985, 138.

6 Graphic design throughout the book is by Chen Pin-Ju.

7 Online. Available at http://www.professays.com/wp-content/uploads/2009/12/Essay-Outline-Sample.gif; http://www.jsd.k12.ak.uk/~daviss/sampleessayoutline.pdf

8 Mark Tredinnick, *Writing Well: The Essential Guide*, Cambridge: Cambridge University Press, 2008, 208.

9 Robin S. Harris and Robert L. McDougall, *The Undergraduate Essay*, Toronto: University of Toronto Press, 1964, 60.

10 Richard Marius, *A Writer's Companion*, 3rd ed., New York: McGraw-Hill, Inc., 1991, 61.

11 G.K. Chesterton, "On Sandals and Simplicity," ed. John Gross, *The Oxford Book of Essays*, Oxford: Oxford University Press, 1991, 377.

12 Martin Corner, "The Novel and Public Truth: Saul Bellow's *The Dean's December*," *Studies in American Fiction*, Vol. 28, No. 1 (Spring 2000), 116-7.

13 John Kenneth Galbraith, *The Affluent Society*, Boston: Mentor Books, 1971, 151.

14 Robin S. Harris and Robert L. McDougall, *The Undergraduate Essay*, University of Toronto Press, Toronto, 1964 (1958), 59-60: "the commonest methods of advancing the arguments of a paragraph: nearly all are variants on one or the other of two basic methods of procedure which are fundamental to all thinking: enumeration, and comparison and contrast. The former is operative in any listing of illustrations or supporting detail, in any attempt at classification, and in any consideration of causes and effects. The latter method, which establishes similarities or differences between objects or ideas, may take the form of definition...elimination...or analogy. In only the simplest of discussions, however, can the argument within a paragraph be handled by a single method. More often than not various methods are used in combination. The more elaborate the chain of thought, or the more numerous and diverse the details within a paragraph, the more varied and subtle the structure is likely to be."

15 Richard Marius, *A Writer's Companion*, 3rd ed., New York: McGraw Hill, Inc., 1991, 55.

16 Mark Tredinnick, *Writing Well: The Essential Guide*, Cambridge: Cambridge University Press, 2008, 226.

17 Richard Marius, *A Writer's Companion*, 3rd ed., New York: Alfred A. Knopf, 1991, 161.

18 John Kay, *Prospect*, "The balance sheet," July 2002, 28.

19 Gavin J. Fairbairn and Christopher Winch, *Reading, Writing and Reasoning: A Guide for Students*, Buckingham and Bristol: The Society for Research and Higher Education and the Open University Press, 1991, 1992, 1993, 25.

20 Andrew Bennett and Nicholas Royle, "Racial Difference," *Introduction to Literature, Theory and Criticism*, Upper Saddler River, New Jersey: Prentice Hall, 1999, 206-7.

21 René Girard, "Myth and Ritual in Shakespeare: *A Midsummer Night's Dream*," *Textual Strategies: Perspectives in Post-Structuralists Criticism*, ed., Josie V. Harari, Ithaca: Cornell University Press, 1999, 193-4.

22 Paul Krugman, "Digital Robber Barons," *The New York Times*, 2002. Online. Available at http://www.nytimes.com/2002/12/06/opinion/digital-robber-barons.html

23 Eric Hobsdawn, "In defence of history," *the Guardian*, 15 January 2005.

24 David Gervais, "The English and the European: the poetry of Geoffrey Hill," *The Revision of Englishness*, eds., David Rogers and John McLeod, Manchester: Manchester University Press, 2004, 65-80.

25 Edward J. Corbett, *Classical Rhetoric for the Modern Student*, 2nd ed., New York: Oxford University Press, 1971, 304-8.

26 Fred J. Cook and Gene Gleason, "He Never Had a Chance," *A View of The Nation: An Anthology*, ed., H.M. Christman, 1959, 152-3, cited in Edward J. Corbett, *Classical Rhetoric for the Modern Student*, 2nd ed., New York: Oxford University Press, 1971, 307-8.

27 Rachel L. Carson, "The Gray Beginnings," *The Sea Around Us*, London: Staples Press Limited, 1951, 3-4.

28 George Orwell, "Politics and the English Language," *The Penguin Essays of George Orwell*, London: Penguin Books, 1994, 248-9.

29 Arnold J. Toynbee, "Does History Repeat Itself?," *Civilisation on Trial*, London: Oxford University Press, 1948, 29-30.

30 Kenneth Tynan, *Curtains: Selections from the Drama Criticism and Related Writings*, New York: Atheneum, 1961, 61-2.

Bibliography

Ashman, Sandra and Phyllis Crème, *How to Write Essays: A Guide for Students*, 3rd ed., London: PNL, 1992.

Barrass, Robert, *Students Must Write: A Guide to Better Writing in Coursework and Examinations*, London and New York: Routledge, 1982, 1995.

Barzun, Jacques, *Simple & Direct: A Rhetoric for Writers*, New York and London: Harper and Rowe Publishers, 1975, 1976.

Brooks, Cleanth and Robert Penn Warren, *Modern Rhetoric*, 3rd ed., New York: Harcourt, Brace & World, 1970.

Clancy, John and Brigid Ballard, *How to Write Essays: A Practical Guide for Students*, Melbourne: Longman Cheshire Pty Limited, 1981, 1983, 1985.

Clark, Matthew, *A Matter of Style: On Writing and Technique*, Oxford and New York: Oxford University Press, 2002.

Corbett, Edward P.J., *Classical Rhetoric for the Modern Student*, 2nd ed., New York: Oxford University Press, 1971.

Creme Phyllis and Mary R. Lea, *Writing at University: A Guide for Students*, Buckingham and Philadelphia: Open University Press, 1997, 1998.

Cuba, Lee and John Cocking, *How to Write About the Social Sciences*, Essex: Addison Wesley Longman, Ltd., 1997.

Elbow, Peter, *Writing with Power: Techniques for Mastering the Writing Process*, New York and Oxford: Oxford University Press, 1981, 1988.

Fabb, Nigel and Alan Durant, *How to Write Essays, Dissertations and Theses in Literary Studies*, London and New York: Longman, 1993.

Fairbairn, Gavin J. and Christopher Winch, *Reading, Writing and Reasoning: A Guide for Students*, Buckingham and Bristol: The Society for Research and Higher Education and the Open University Press, 1991, 1992, 1993.

Freedman Sarah, ed., *The Acquisition of Written Language: Response and Revision*, Freedman, Norwood, NJ: Ablex Publishing Corporation, 1985.

Gibaldi, Joseph, *MLA Handbook for Research Papers*, 6th ed., New York: MLA, 2003.

Greenbaum, Sidney, *An Introduction to English Grammar*, Harlow: Longman, 1991.

Greetham, Brya, *How to Write Better Essays*, Basingstoke and New York: Palgrave, 2001.

Griffith, Kelly, *Writing Essays about Literature: A Guide and Style Sheet*, 5th ed., London: Harcourt Brace College Publishers, 1998.

Gross, John, ed., *The Oxford Book of Essays*, Oxford: Oxford University Press, 1991.

Harris, Robin S. and Robert L. McDougall, *The Undergraduate Essay*, Toronto: University of Toronto Press, 1964.

Kane, Thomas S., *The New Oxford Guide to Writing*, New York and Oxford: Oxford University Press, 1998.

Kurlich, Frances and Helen Whitaker, *Writing Strategies for Student Writers*, New York: Holt, Rinehart & Winston, Inc., 1988.

Lanham, Richard A., *Style: An Anti-Texbook*, New Haven and London: Yale University Press, 1974.

Lanham, *Analyzing Prose*, 2nd ed., London: Continuum, 2003.

Lanham, *Revising Prose*, 5th ed., London: Longman, 2007.

Lea, Mary and Barry Stierer, eds., *Student Writing in Higher Education: New Contexts*, Buckingham and Philadelphia: The Society for Research and Higher Education and the Open University Press, 2000.

Marius, Richard, *A Writer's Companion*, 3rd ed., New York: Alfred A. Knopf, 1991.

Meriwether, Nell W., *Strategies for Writing Successful Essays*, Lincolnwood, Illinois: NCT Publishing Group, 1997.

Mills, Paul, *Writing in Action*, London and New York: Routledge, 1996.

Pinnells, Jim, *Writing: Process and Structure*, London: Harper & Row, Publishers, 1998.

Redman, Peter, *Good Essay Writing: A Social Science Guide*, London: Sage Publications (with the Open University), 2001.

Roberts, David, *The Student's Guide to Writing Essays*, London: Kogan Page, 1997.

Rose, Jean, *The Mature Student's Guide to Writing*, Basingstoke: Palgrave, 2001.

Stott, R. *et al.*, eds., *Making your Case: A Practical Guide to Essay Writing*, London: Longman, 2001.

Taylor, Gordon, *The Student's Writing Guide for the Arts and Social Sciences*, Cambridge: Cambridge University Press, 1989, 90, 92.

Trask, R.L., *Penguin Guide to Punctuation*, London: Penguin, 1997.

Tredinnick, Mark, *Writing Well: The Essential Guide*, Cambridge, Cambridge University Press, 2008.

Warburton, Nigel, *The Basics of Essay Writing*, London and New York: Routledge, 2006.

Williams, Kate, *Writing Essays*, Oxford: Oxford Centre for Staff Development, 1995.

Appendix

Overall Stages in Our Writing Process for Argumentative Essays

1. **The Procrastination Stage:** Incorporate whatever form of procrastination puts you in the right frame of mind to begin writing.

2. **The Freewriting Stage:** Set aside around 30 minutes and write with abandon about your topic. Then take a break.

3. **The Planning Stage:** Reread your freewriting and then organize the ideas, trying not to become too attached to your plan.

4. **The Mastermind Stage:** Compose a mastermind draft, writing or typing yourself to a conclusion.

5. **The Argumentative or Persuasive Stage:** Copy the conclusion at the end of your mastermind draft and paste it at the beginning.

6. **The Weighty Stage – Thesis Statements:** Revise your newly pasted conclusion into a more effective thesis.

7. **The Content Stage – Paragraphing:** Substantiate and refine the content of your essay and check your style.

8. **The Stylish Stage – Formal Introductory Paragraphs:** Insert one of the four most common types of formal introductory paragraphs (or combination of types) before your thesis statement.

9. **The Refinement Stage:** Reread your essay and then your thesis a final time. Check your spelling and punctuation.

Instructor's Guide

I have designed *Writing Better Essays* to serve as a text on composition courses for university students, although it should be accessible to anyone who is interested in improving her essay writing skills. The central aim of the book is to provide uncomplicated stages to help students develop a reliable process of writing and drafting argumentative essays that requires no formal training or experience with rhetoric and that follows from what they probably do naturally. The book emphasizes structure and coherence, most centrally through explanations of the similarity between the structure of spoken and written attempts at persuasion and the importance of students' understanding how to generate ideas through better paragraphing. To achieve these concepts, I have explained each of the individual stages for the process in detail, provided accompanying exercises, and listed examples of good practice for students to imitate. Imitation and simple rhetorical techniques and devices form the basis of the methodology of the book and its instruction.

The most effective way for instructors to use the book is to assign chapters and accompanying exercises on a week-by-week or class-by-class basis, if possible, and to devote class time to discussions of the explanations in the book of such elements as mastermind drafts, thesis statements, and paragraphs. By the end of a semester or a course term, students will have been able to create a portfolio of exercises and imitations as well as a log of good practice gleaned from their own reading. They will have composed an argumentative essay, having taken it through a series of stages and drafts, after each of which ideally they will have had formative feedback from an instructor and/or fellow classmates. As a consequence, they will have experienced firsthand the benefits of drafting their essays as well as the benefits of "apeing" best practice rather than having just been informed of concepts in the abstract. They should also have begun to acquire the confidence and self-discipline necessary to continue to practice their new-found skills on their own in the future and to utilize a process for writing their essays, either by the one that the book provides or one they have adapted from it.

The key to being able to develop such confidence and self-discipline is practice, however, and practicing anything without support and guidance is never easy. Even the most determined students might struggle to practice often enough to ensure genuine improvement. Students will therefore benefit enormously from the encouragement and experience of an instructor who can help them to acquire and sustain the discipline needed to repeat the exercises involving imitation, which can understandably seem tedious initially. My experience has shown, however, that, when students perform these imitation exercises, they soon appreciate the value of experiencing the qualities of good writing for themselves. They recognize ticks in their own style more readily, and they improve.

Nowhere are the exercises of imitation more crucial than in the book's chapter on paragraphs. The chapter focuses on ways to help students generate the many supporting ideas that often lie unrecognized within the general assertions that characterize their essays. I have risked a long explanation of different types of paragraphs and a demonstration of ways of developing effective ones from typical student examples, for, if novice writers understand the principles behind good paragraphs and learn to apply them, they should be able to write good argumentative essays. The examples for imitation come from a wide range of disciplines, and I hope that students will find the content of the paragraphs interesting for its own sake. The selections should, among other qualities, also illustrate the consistency with which professional writers typically explain their ideas more thoroughly, more methodically, and more coherently than aspiring writers. Having an instructor explain these examples, as well as encourage students to imitate them carefully, perhaps through formal assignments, and to get into the habit of identifying good practice in their reading, will help their understanding considerably.

This book may seem prescriptive in some of its recommendations, including its encouragement for students to err on the side of reiteration and explicit transitional devices, its advice to students to take a reductionist approach to punctuation, and its central emphasis on the mastermind draft as the fulcrum of the writing process. However, this strategy rests on the fact that many, if not most, students will not have had much previous instruction in grammar or punctuation and may have been left to devise their own process for writing essays. From my experience, their reaction to the latter is to rely on a single draft of their essays that leads them to a conclusion, which is useful for the process that the book proposes, but a conclusion that is usually unanticipated and/or not developed coherently from the analysis that comprises the body of their essays. Rather than ask students to change this tack completely, however, the book turns their existing practice into an integral part of their writing process. The rationale is that students need to gain confidence with a new method that is familiar and fairly easy to use and that works in a self-fulfilling way if they are going to embrace it and its chief premise: that they must draft their essays extensively.

Once students show that they understand the fundamentals of structure and coherence that make up that process and can apply those same fundamentals in their essays, then they should certainly be encouraged to experiment, to create their own processes, and develop their own styles. The prescriptions in the book, in other words, are only provisional. They may provide students, in whatever context, with an accessible and practical foundation upon which they can build, regardless of their educational background, their previous training in essay writing, and/or their formal understanding of punctuation.

Lightning Source UK Ltd.
Milton Keynes UK
UKOW03f1556130714

234989UK00002B/13/P